Tarot Forecast 2009

Your Yearly, Monthly and Weekly Prediction
with Remedies

CAPRICORN

(December 22 to January 19)

Dr. Seema Mid.

HEALTH HARMONY

An imprint of

B. Jain Publishers (P) Ltd.

An ISO 9001 : 2000 Certified Company
USA – Europe – India

TAROT FORECAST 2009

First Edition: 2008

All rights reserved. No part of this book may be reproduced, stored in a retrieval system or transmitted, in any form or by any means, mechanical, photocopying, recording or otherwise, without any prior written permission of the publisher.

© with the author

Published by Kuldeep Jain for

HEALTH HARMONY

An imprint of
B. JAIN PUBLISHERS (P) LTD.
An ISO 9001 : 2000 certified Company
1921/10, Chuna Mandi, Paharganj, New Delhi 110 055 (INDIA)
Tel.: 91-11-2358 0800, 2358 1100, 2358 1300, 2358 3100
Fax: 91-11-2358 0471 *Email:* info@bjain.com
Website: **www.bjainbooks.com**

Printed in India by
J.J. Offset Printers

ISBN: 978-81-319-0658-3

CONTENTS

Publisher's Note 5

Acknowledgement 7

Introduction to Tarot 9

Spreads 12

About the Book 14

Capricorn Personality 19

Year 2009 for you 21

Monthly Prediction 2009 26

Weekly Prediction 2009 36

Remedies 162

PUBLISHER'S NOTE

With immense pleasure we are introducing this book on 'Tarot Forecast 2009'. Today Tarot science is at its best and people are using its benefits in different ways and modes.

Here we present one of the best solutions offered by Tarot that is prediction of future with the help of Tarot cards. It determines what all can happen in the times coming ahead. This information can be used to mould the things for better results and ways. Not only that, Tarot gives you an insight into obstacles & their best possible solutions. With her knowledge & experience Dr. Seema Midha gives advices and remedies to fight such instances.

Dr. Seema Midha is Asia's one of the famous Tarot card readers and one of the bestselling author of 'Mystical Tarot Deck'. We hope our readers will be benefited by this forecast and enjoy life by referring it.

Kuldeep Jain
CEO, B. Jain Publishers

ACKNOWLEDGEMENT

First and foremost, I would like to thank God Almighty, without whom anything would have not been possible. I am blessed to have such a great family who has been supportive throughout all my endeavors and feats. I would like to thank my publisher who have had the faith in me and given me this wonderful opportunity to come up with this amazing idea. They have been my support system, always showering me with love and giving me the strength to move on and achieve success in whatever I pursue. I would also like to extend my thanks to Aishwarya Ganesh, who helped me a lot. I am truly blessed to be surrounded by such an extraordinary people in my life.

INTRODUCTION TO TAROT

Tarot which is pronounced as 'Taro' refers to the Royal Path. It is a spiritual journey which consists of 78 cards which contains different objects, colours, numbers and symbols. All these cards need to be understood and interpreted so as to get guidance. Tarot reading communicates the meaning because we bring to them our sincere desire to discover deeper truths about our lives.

All cards have different meanings which need to be understood and are related to the situations so as to get meaningful conclusion. Tarot cards prove very helpful when people are in need and dilemma. These cards guide us and prepare us for the coming obstacles in our lives. These are the tools which when believed can change our lives drastically for the positive.

Tarot is a science which helps us sail through the coming obstacles whether day to day or major life problems regarding relations, career, education, job or marriage. Tarot gives positive energy and confidence to face the conflicts that we all face in our everyday lives. Thus, tarot cards help us to emerge as more powerful, strong and a more confident person.

The Tarot deck consists of 78 cards which are classified into major arcana which contains 22 cards and minor arcana containing 56 cards.

The minor arcana is further divided into 4 suits of 14 cards each consisting of 10 pip cards from Ace to Ten and four courts- Page, Knight, Queen and King.

The four suits are Wands, Cups, Swords and Pentacles.

Wands is a fire element card representing ability and determination and the will to succeed.

Swords is an air element card representing forces working against you.

Cups is a water element card representing forces working for you.

Pentacles is an earth element card representing influence of material possessions and monetary benefits.

1. **Pentacles:** Earth element and feminine energy show abundance, prosperity, material, fertility, cultivation, divine path (spirituality) and wealth.
2. **Wands:** Fire held by masculine hands show work that we do, career, progress, fire, zeal, fire burns and progress in work.
3. **Cups:** Water element shows feminine energy that comes from clouds, love, emotions, relationships and partnerships.
4. **Swords:** Air energy indicates mind, thought and intellect. Sword cuts thought in the air. Sometimes, thinking or thought process can also be killing.

INTRODUCTION TO TAROT / 11

Wands – Red and Brown
Cups- Blue and Green
Swords- Cream and Grey
Pentacles- Green and Yellow
Major arcana- Purple and White

We are using our Mystical Tarot Deck for the year 2009 prediction for every Zodiac Sign. The method has been given in sequence.

SPREADS

We use different spreads for different questions. If you want to analyze a specific question in depth, we use specific spreads. We start with the yearly prediction. We explain you how we have provided with our prediction.

Yearly prediction

We start-of by taking out one card representing the overall year prediction for a particular Zodiac Sign. Then, we take out 12 more cards indicating, 12 months for that sign. Later we pick up 5 cards indicating different aspects such as health, money, relations, career and guidance.

Monthly prediction

Then, we pick up 4 different cards indicating each week of the month. Thus, there are 48 cards drawn for 12 months.

Weekly prediction

After the yearly and the monthly predictions, we move on to the weekly prediction. There are 53 weeks in a year. The weekly prediction consists of 13 cards. We take out 1 card indicating the whole week, then 7 different cards indicating each day in that particular week. After the week is over, we draw five more cards each representing:

1. Love
2. Money
3. Health
4. Career, and
5. Education

Also, we have included lucky colours, lucky numbers, lucky days and remedies which can be followed so as to make the week luckier and beneficial.

By this you can come to know how you can take up the opportunity that knocks at your door and also take care of the negative things that can affect you by making the remedial changes.

ABOUT THE BOOK

In this book, we have given you the yearly, monthly and weekly predictions for Capricorn for the year 2009.

Along with the weekly prediction, we have also provided you with the lucky colours, lucky numbers, lucky days and the remedies in each weekly prediction.

The lucky colours suggest that you shall use the given colour in your daily routine by any means during that week. Different colours help you in enhancing your strength, courage, stability, energy, etc.

For example- The usage of Red colour in our routine gives us vibrant energy, and enthusiasm.

Yellow colour gives us courage and strength.

Pink colour enhances our relations with our loved ones.

The lucky numbers suggest that in a particular week, you shall work with those people whose date of birth matches with the numbers prescribed. Lucky numbers help and guide, for example, when we work with our colleagues, we can deal and mingle with those whose date of birth matches with the lucky number.

People who are planning to buy a house, property or car can buy using these numbers, etc.

The lucky days suggest that you shall complete or initiate new work on the days mentioned. You can plan any trip on these lucky days. If you are buying any car, or any other property on these lucky days, it will prove to be very auspicious.

This helps you to be more prosperous and more confident regarding the task being undertaken.

The remedies which have been mentioned helps you to prepare yourself for the obstacles that may arise and they help you to enhance yourself so that you can enjoy the week even better. A list of remedies has been given at the end of the book.

CAPRICORN

(December 22 to January 19)

Your Element: Earth
Your Ruling Planet: Saturn
Symbol: The Goat
Your Stone: Garnet
Life Pursuit: To be proud of their achievements
Vibration: Powerful resilient energy
Capricorn Secret Desire: To be admired by their family, friends and the world at large

apricorns are very down to earth and cautious. They are found to be very hard working and they believe in achieving their dreams. They usually end up successfully in the things they do. They might lack self-confidence and self-esteem sometimes. Although Capricorns are found to be very affectionate and humorous, they first like to know the people and then get close to them. By nature, Capricorns are cautious when entering in to a new love relationship, but once they feel safe with their partner, the cool exterior melts away to reveal a sensitive and loyal heart beneath. They like to work quietly and effectively and in this process they tend to forget themselves.

It's very hard for people belonging to this sun sign to trust a stranger. They like to work in a practical and methodical way to achieve what they desire. They are very particular about planning for the future as they always want a material and financial security in their days to come. Some qualities which they possess are commitment, hard-working, frugal and resourceful. The natural quality of commitment makes them successful in the things they attempt. They believe in the philosophy of self-sufficiency and do not bother to ask others to carry them. They show perfection in their work and their ambitious nature always motivates them.

Being trustworthy to themselves, they expect the same from others. The ruling planet for the Capricorns is Saturn. The people with this sign get success, happiness and power in life. They are natural orators, teachers and deep thinkers. The people under this sign are devotees to book knowledge and worshippers of the intellect. The women with this sign prove to be more discreet financial managers rather than the men.

The Capricorns hate flattery. They are sometimes selfish and can become cruel in their denunciation. They reach their goals because they know the longest journey commences with a single step and that the first step is always the most difficult. Even if something comes to a grinding halt, their ambition to reach the ultimate keeps them moving forever onwards and upwards.

CAPRICORN

YEAR 2009 FOR YOU

Overall
'Seven of cups' indicates that this year you will be very happy and satisfied emotionally, personally and professionally. The year 2009 is indicating a prosperous time when you will get everything what you want.

Health
'Ten of Pentacles' says that the year 2009 will be fine as far as your health is concerned. You may face minor health ailments which you need to give proper attention, so that it does not take the shape of major health problems. You will have to be action oriented this year.

Money
'The World' says that you will be able to fulfil all your material and monetary desires. You have the ability and capabilities which are needed to fulfil your dreams.

Relations
'The Justice' says that the year 2009 will bring in justice and rewards as far as your relations are concerned.

This is a very prosperous and a happy time to start new relations.

Career
'The Chariot' says that now you have started the journey towards the attainment of more knowledge. You will achieve what you want in your career because of your determination and the will to gain more knowledge. Students planning to go for higher studies have a bright chance.

Guidance
'The Star' says that you will be blessed and shown the correct path by God without much delay or obstacles. You will be shining as a bright star wherever you go this year. New journey is indicated this year.

MONTHLY OVERVIEW 2009

January
'Eight of Pentacles' says that you will be possessive at the start of the month. You will earn money but you need to share this money with others so that you can help them in different ways.

February
'Five of Swords' says that in this month, you will be taking on all the responsibilities at a time battling with all the obstacles. You have to set all the things correctly instead making a mess out of it.

March
'The Page of Swords' says that you will be full of zeal and energy but you need to have full knowledge regarding the path you undertake. You need to consult and receive prior guidance from people who are experienced and then implement your plans. This month you will be full of enthusiasm.

April
'Seven of Wands' says that you continue doing your hard work and putting in your efforts. You will face the fruitful results soon if you keep working like this. This month will be very action oriented

May
'Queen of Cups' says that you will be fully emotional this month. You will be taking decisions using your heart instead of your mind. You should not let others take your advantage as you are deeply attached with your surroundings. You need to behave in a more strong and matured way this month.

June
In the month of June, 'Five of Wands' brings in competition and more hard work so as to accomplish which may be difficult but not impossible. You need to take up the challenge and face it with determination so that you get to prove yourself in front of others

July
'Three of Wands' says that you will continue enjoying the high position in this month too. You will be more inclined towards attaining knowledge. This is a month when you can learn more things

August
'King of Pentacles' says that you will enjoy a very commendable position this month. You should not take advantage of your position and misuse it. In this month you will gain monetary benefits from unexpected sources.

September
'Page of Pentacles' says that your high energy and

passion to complete your work will not go waste this month. You are rearing and desperate to achieve your goal leading to monetary benefits too.

October
'Four of Swords' says that this is the correct time to surrender yourself so that you are able to give more attention to your work.

November
In the month of November, you will experience lot of gains from share market, lottery or property. A financially high period for all of you.

December
'Four of Cups' says that in this month you will be less action-oriented, thinking deeply about the situations. You may be busy, thinking about the past, which was to be forgotten long back. There are offers in front of you which you have to accept and move ahead.

MONTHLY PREDICTION 2009

JANUARY
'Eight of Pentacles' says that you will be possessive at the start of the month. You will earn money but you need to share this money with others so that you can help them in different ways.

In the first week, 'Queen of Wands' says that you will be high on your career. You will enjoy your success and be on a high throughout the week. In the second week, 'the Moon' says that due to the achievement you attained last week, you may get egoistic and doubtful. In this way, your attitude will lead some third person to overtake you. You need to be cautious so that you move in the right direction. In the third week, 'the High Priestess says that you are very intelligent and bright but you need to utilize this brightness in the right direction. In the fourth week, 'Page of Cups' says that you will be high on emotions and this will give you high energy and enthusiasm. You will be now on the right track.

FEBRUARY
'Five of Swords' says that in this month, you will be taking on all the responsibilities at a time battling with all the obstacles. You have to set all the things correctly instead of making a mess out of it.

In the first week, you will be focused and determined

knowing the path to your destination. You may feel a bit stagnant but you will overcome that situation soon. In the second week, 'Queen of Pentacles' suggests that this week, you will earn monetary benefits. You shall go for shopping avoiding over expenditure. You need to make better plans so as to take initiatives for future security. In the third week, 'the Judgment card' says that you will wait and watch for results to come. Students may get to hear positive results. This is a very positive week for all of you. In the fourth week, The 'Wheel of Fortune' says that there may be some ups and downs at the career front. But you need to understand that you need to face these tough circumstances in order to rise. Everything will take a positive shape in the near future.

MARCH

'The Page of Swords' says that you will be full of zeal and energy but you need to have full knowledge regarding the path you undertake. You need to consult and get prior guidance from people who are experienced and then implement your plans. This month you will be full of enthusiasm.

In the first week, you will have to take the help of manipulation so that your work gets done. You may not be able to complete a project without the help of someone. Take his/her help and you will achieve the much needed success. In the second week, you will see the face of completion. All pending work will come to a positive end. This is a very good time to initiate new projects too. In the third week, 'the Hermit' says that this week you will concentrate on showing light and guidance to others. You may feel a bit sad and hurt because they may not be very interested to listen and put your words to action. You need to use your energy to your own use. In the fourth week, 'Ten of Wands' says that you will be over-loaded with extra pressure and work. This week, you need to take proper care of your health.

APRIL

'Seven of Wands' says that you continue doing your hard work and putting in your efforts. You will face the fruitful results soon if you keep on working like this. This month will be very action-oriented.

In the first week, you take out some time for charity work. You will concentrate on helping others with the resources you have. In the second week, 'Page of Wands' says that you are full of energy and enthusiastic attitude will definitely show you the correct path. Students will have the courage and passion to do something new. In the third week, 'the Hanged Man' says that after a full passionate month, you will now be in a state of confusion. You may not know which path to be undertaken. But you need to have faith and trust in

God. He will definitely show you the road out of this tough situation. In the last week, 'Seven of Pentacles' says that you need to be more action-oriented and re invest the money you have accumulated till now. Overall, you will experience a good month.

MAY

'Queen of Cups' says that you will be fully emotional this month. You will be taking decisions using your heart, instead of your mind. You should not let others take your advantage as you are deeply attached with your surroundings. You need to behave in a more strong and matured way this month.

In the first week, 'the Temperance' says you will balance your karmic deeds. You will be able to maintain your focus and willpower in the job you accomplish. In the second week, 'Eight of Swords' says that there is a blind fold on your eyes. This may be because you trust someone very deeply. But you need to be independent and take decisions using the resources you have in front of you. In the third week, 'the Death card' implies that there will be a complete revolution or a re-birth that you will experience either at the wok place or at home. People will see you as a changed person and as a new person. During this time, you need to take the changes positively. In the fourth week, 'the Sun Card' says that you will outshine others in every respect. You will gain more respect and fame for yourself now.

JUNE

In the month of June, 'Five of Wands' brings in competition and more hard work so as to accomplish, which may be difficult but not impossible. You need to take up the challenge and face it with determination so that you get to prove yourself in front of others.

'Three of Swords' says that in the first week, in order to outshine others you may create some obstacles for yourself. You have to tackle each situation individually. The second week, says that 'the Emperor' brings in intellect and spirituality. You will start taking unnecessary tensions while taking care of others. In this process you are neglecting yourself. You need to take care of your health, because if you are healthy then only you will be able to serve others. The third week brings in a high position for you. You will be high on career. Students will see positive results in their examinations. Office-going people will see an increase in their post. In the fourth week, 'Eight of Cups' says that you will start getting detached from your emotions and relations. Your concentration will change from emotions to career. This is a month when you will enjoy a high position.

JULY

'Three of Wands' says that you will continue enjoying the high position in this month too. You will be more inclined towards attaining knowledge. This is a month when you can learn more things.

In the first week, 'Knight of Wands' says that your zeal, passion and power is now pushing you to be more energetic and as a result you will start moving on the right track towards your destination. In the second week, 'Nine of Pentacles' says that you now get to earn and enjoy the fruits of your focus and determination. This is a very prosperous time, whether it will be career, job, or home. A highly enjoyable time is now on its way. In the third week, 'Five of Pentacles' says you may get a setback or suffer a loss due to your inability to manage the finances properly. You need to take proper steps so that you can avoid this situation. In the fourth week, 'Empress' says that now you will be giving and sharing what you have with others. You will be happy serving others. You can even do some charity work for the poor, old people or children.

AUGUST

'King of Pentacles' says that you will enjoy a very commendable position this month. You should not take advantage of your position and misuse it. In this month you will gain monetary benefits from unexpected sources.

In the first week, you will see yourself ready and rearing to go ahead beating all others in the race. You will be very fast in taking decisions. You need to slow down and take steps wisely. In the second week, 'Ace of Cups' says that you will be highly emotional and sentimental. There are chances of you getting in a love affair or attracted to someone. In the third week, 'Nine of Cups' says that you will be highly content and satisfied with your emotional wellbeing. In the fourth week, the 'Queen of Swords' says that you will put your intellect and energy to use. But in a situation there are both negative and positive aspects which need to be analyzed properly to get accurate conclusions.

SEPTEMBER

'Page of Pentacles' says that your high energy and passion to complete your work will not go waste this month. You are rearing and desperate to achieve your goal leading to monetary benefits too.

At the start of the month, 'the Knight of Pentacles' indicates that your work may get stagnant as you are not putting in the right inputs. You need to invest money at this point of time so that you take a step forward. In the second week, you will have an improvement seeing yourself touching new heights. You will come as a winner and be very delighted and happy. In the third week, you will see yourself getting lonely and aloof. You have to meet more people so that there is exchange of ideas and views. You will be able to progress if you are open to people and loved ones. In the fourth week, 'Six of Swords' says that the obstacles you face will disappear, as you will tackle them with intelligence using your experiences as guiding forces.

OCTOBER

'Four of Swords' says that this is the correct time to surrender yourself so that you are able to give more attention to your work.

In the first week, 'Two of Pentacles' says you will see offers and money coming and going from your hands. This is a time when you are able to balance your work. In the second week, 'Three of Cups' indicates that socially a very high and an enjoyable time is coming your way. You can plan reunions, get togethers with friends, and relive all old memories. In the third week, you will gain material and financial benefits. This is the correct time to plan investment in properties. In the fourth week, 'Ten of Swords' says that people are likely to take advantage of you. You may even come in other peoples words and take up their responsibilities by forgetting your work.

NOVEMBER

In the month of November you will experience lot of gains from share market, lottery or property. A financially high period for all of you.

In the first week of November, you will be inside a frame, making assumptions for yourself. You shall not

34 / CAPRICORN

make terms and conditions for yourself. It can ruin the situations for you. You need to mix up with people exchanging ideas and views so that you are able to satisfy your emotional and esteem needs. In the second week, 'Four of Cups' says that you will be sad due to a setback suffered. You shall not be depressed as every day has new hope in itself. You should take the next step in life with the things you have in hand forgetting the past. In the third week, 'the Lovers' bring an emotional bonding with a special person. You will get attracted to someone at the office or at a social gathering. A highly enjoyable time is there in store for you. In the last week, 'the Devil' says that negative vibrations from people may have an effect on you. You need to understand people and stay away from those who can take advantage of you. You have to be highly positive in this month.

DECEMBER

'Four of Cups' says that in this month you will be less action-oriented, thinking deeply about the situations. You may be busy thinking about the past which was to be forgotten long back. There are offers in front of you which you have to accept and move ahead.

In the first week, you will see yourself using all the resources in the right direction. You will be highly focused and determined. In the second week, the 'Knight of Cups' says that, you are emotional, intelligent and focused towards your goal. The environment around you is also supportive and you will get the much-needed guidance from your loved ones. In the third week, 'Two of Cups' says that you are likely to shift your concentration to your loved ones. You will get full support from your partner. A plan or a journey can also be planned during this time. In the fourth week, 'King of Swords' says that your intellect and analytical power are being utilized fully. You will be evaluative and speculative about the situations around you. Overall, this month will be high on emotions and you need to enjoy the month fully.

WEEKLY PREDICTION 2009

1st Week
(December 28 to January 3)

Overview

'The Temperance' says that this week, you will be able to maintain a strike between all your chores and relations. This week people around you will be happy with the way you work and manage all your responsibilities. You will be the centre of discussion at the work place and at home. You have everything in front of you, but these things are worth only when they are fully utilized. You need to open your eyes and take full advantage of these elements. Do not make any decision in a hurry or immaturity. You have to be practical and take the help of your seniors and elders for major decisions. You will be highly energetic this week. A journey is indicated this week. You will be concentrating and focusing on the work allotted to you. You will achieve success in this project. At the personal front too, you will be very satisfied. You have to be bold and strong while facing the situations. Do not be indecisive, whenever you need help, consult your loved ones and elders. They will be able to show you the right path. As the week comes to an end, you will be highly emotional but strong and very cheerful. You need to get engrossed and focus on the work, which has been assigned to you. Then only you will achieve your goals on time.

Love
'The Hermit' indicates that you will be content with your personal life, you need to spend more time with your partner so as to give them a chance to express their feelings too. You need to divert your attention to your home too.

Money
You will secure lots of gains, which give a sense of achievement, and satisfaction and this will be possible through your hard work and willingness to work.

Health
'Nine of Pentacles' indicates that you will be highly satisfied and content with your life. Thus, you will enjoy and be happy. Health will be excellent this week

Career
'Knight of Cups' says that you will be interested to take up new and different projects this week. You want to move ahead and take the next step.

Education
This week, you have to keep your jealousy and ego aside so as to move ahead. Do not think about others, instead concentrate on your aim, this will be beneficial for you.

Lucky numbers
7 and 9

Lucky colour
White

Lucky days
Sunday, Monday and Wednesday

Remedies
You need to take decisions on time by listening to others too and accepting their ideas. You have to deal with maturity and practicality with the situations. There is a need to learn more things about the environment too. You are not giving much importance to relationships which need a lot of time, space and respect. This week, you have to fulfill the needs and wants of your family. You need to change your dominating attitude and be calmer.

2nd Week
(January 4 to 10)

Overview
'Five of Swords' says that our energy may compel you to try your hand at every opportunity. But, you need to be practical and choose only that option where your interest lies. You need to have perfection in all work.

You will reach your aim on time. People will know you and you will be recognized. This is a good time to enjoy and have a blast. You will be willing and energetic to work more. Your aim is fixed and you will definitely achieve it on time. You have lot of gains coming your way. You have to make plans to invest this gain in the proper areas so as to benefit more. Do not get possessive. You are trying to cut down from everyone, hence being alone and aloof. You have to be among people and be interactive. Project your ideas and thoughts and also welcome suggestions from others. You are tending to get possessive, as you are not spending the money wherever needed. You have to spend some of this money on your relatives and satisfy their needs on time. You will be back by yourself and people will enjoy your company. You will be able to enjoy each and every minute of life. You will get all that you desire. You will be on top as the king of the world.

Love
'Page of Wands' indicates that you will be highly enthusiastic and.this is the perfect time to start on new relations.

Money
This is the apt and the perfect time to make future investments or buy property. You will get high returns

from these investments, as you are idle; hence, you have to be action oriented.

Health
Your health will be fine this week as you are regularly taking good care.

Career
'King of Cups' indicates that you will get authority and power at the office. You are likely to get new assignments, which will match your qualifications.

Education
You will now be willing to take new classes so as to enhance your knowledge. You are on the right track, but you need to maintain a slow pace.

Lucky numbers
1 and 8

Lucky colour
Grey

Lucky days
Monday, Friday and Saturday

Remedies
There are the need for investments this week. You have everything but you may not be happy and satisfied. You need to get detached with your surroundings so that you are able to focus well. You need to spend time

and help a needy. This will give you mental satisfaction. You need to give and take back at the same time. You will be able to bring back a smile on everybody's face due to your appreciable work, which in return will boost your strength and happiness.

3rd Week
(January 11 to 17)

Overview
'Ten of Wands' indicates that you are likely to overload yourself by taking all the responsibilities on your own shoulders. You have to share and delegate these tasks so that others also get a chance to take up new assignments. You have to make proper utilization of the incoming money, so that your future will get secured. Invest this money at the right time. You will get all the blessings from the divine powers and you will lead a successful content life. You will get more offers coming and going your way. You may even get proposal regarding relationships. 'The Strength' says that you will have to be tactful and manipulative so as to get your work done. Diplomacy will help you solve disagreements, if any. You will be willing to share your belongings with others. People around you will seek your guidance and help. You may face some obstacles in your way, but you will be able to tackle your way out

with diplomacy and experience. You will get all the advantage and move ahead with vigor and courage.

Love
You will be highly energetic and enthusiastic as far as your personal life is concerned. You are likely to get positive response.

Money
'Ace of Pentacles' says that this is a highly prosperous time for money matters. You can receive stuck money this week.

Health
You will be active this week, as you are likely to get a lot of work. Health will be good.

Career
Career needs time and focus. Your mind is elsewhere and as a result you are unable to concentrate on your career.

Education
You have to take up the initiative in order to make the next move, otherwise delays can hamper your target. This week you have to make investment in the needed area.

Lucky numbers
5 and 6

Lucky colour
Lemon Yellow

Lucky days
Monday, Thursday and Saturday

Remedies
A balance between your work and personal life is needed. You need to have the patience while handling different situations. Do not act or react in a hurry, you can get hurt, as you are not moving ahead. You need to keep aside your immaturity and child-like behaviour. You have to slow down as only the slow and steady wins the race. Do not overload yourself as then you will be unable to finish the projects without perfection. You will get positive results if you follow this remedy.

4th Week
(January 18 to 24)

Overview
'The Tower' says that there has been enough of sacrificing till now. Sometimes you have to live for yourself too. Be independent and try to focus on your tasks, otherwise, you can fall down from your current position. You need to avoid people who have negative attitude. You have to be positive and move on without thinking about the results. You can become highly

motivated regarding a person or task. You will be highly energetic and moving towards your aim with full determination. You can become negative and highly emotional. You should take decisions using your mind instead of heart. Do not trust anybody blindly. Trust your intuition. You will experience an occasion and you will be in a celebration mood. Enjoy to the fullest with your friends and family. 'Two of Wands' indicates that you are highly intelligent and using your mind in the right direction. Take guidance from others during this week. You are likely to become highly spiritual. You have to be a determined decision maker. Do not get confused, but stick to your principles. 'Nine of Swords' says that confusions and conflicts can take a toll on you. You have to open up and welcome suggestions from others. Spend some time with your family so that you do not get stressed out.

Love
Your personal life will be on a smooth platform. You will enjoy the time you spend with your family.

Money
You are moving away from the emotional bondages, but this can even be harmful. In this way, you may not be able to concentrate on your relations too. Be in touch with your family relatives.

Health
You may face minor health problems but you will be able to cure them by proper medication.

Career
'The Lovers' says that career will be smoothly going forward as you are passionate about your work.

Education
'Queen of Pentacles' says that you will get many offers to up-grade your education and knowledge. Do not get showy this week. Be grounded.

Lucky numbers
7 and 3

Lucky colour
Black

Lucky days
Monday, Wednesday and Thursday

Remedies
Your attitude is going in the negative way as you are being rigid and inflexible. For 40 days, visit the temple and pray for yourself and for your loved one's well being. You can even light up Incense sticks. This will enhance and purify the environment and you will see a positive change in your thought process. Your money prospects does not seem fine. You have to stop sacrificing and move ahead in a more confident and bold way.

5th Week
(January 25 to 31)

Overview

'Four of Cups' says that you have to come out of the past feelings and bitter experiences. Then only you will be able to see the present and realize what you have in hand. Accept the best offer that comes your way. You need to surrender yourself totally to the task you have undertaken. You will get a lot of time to enjoy with family and friends. You will have a great and a highly enjoyable time with your close ones. After the celebrations, you will be all yourself by not expressing your feelings to others. You have to be interactive during the mid-week. You will gain a lot of monetary benefits this week giving you pleasure and satisfaction. You will be able to balance your karmic deeds by being spiritual. The Moon' says that you need to keep aside your ego and doubting nature in order to move ahead. You will be content and satisfied with your life route. You will get emotional satisfaction and mental peace at the end of the week.

Love

'Ace of Wands' says that you will be experiencing a high in your personal life. Singles can even meet their soul mates this week.

Money
You will be highly excited about the gains and inflow of money. You will not hesitate in helping others.

Health
You can invite health problems for yourself by not taking care of yourself. You have to be careful this week, and any minor ailments need to be medicated upon.

Career
You are likely to be sad with the progress of your career line. But you have to continue working so as to gain all the way.

Education
You will be helping out your friends with your experience and intellect. They will be pleased with your efforts.

Lucky numbers
4 and 9

Lucky colour
Cream

Lucky days
Monday, Wednesday and Thursday

Remedies
You need to make a list of people who are close to you and call them one by one. This will help you enhance and improve your relations. You have to set your

priorities this week and handle the tasks carefully. You should be happy and move on with life. You can even plan an outing with your friends and refresh your memories of old times. This will be energizing and refreshing.

6th Week
(February 1 to 7)

Overview
You know your negative and positive points and you are ready to work upon them to race ahead. You need not spend the whole money, which has been earned. You shall save some amount for the future by curtailing unnecessary expenses. You will gain a new experience or money with the help of a third person. This third person will be very helpful and beneficial for you. Though you have every element in front of you, you may not be able to realize, as there can be a black-swirl around you. You have to remove the black-swirl and move ahead by utilizing all these benefits. You will be a helping hand to everyone around you. People will be seeking your help and guidance. This in turn will give you a high positive force and energy, which will give you a push and you will definitely take the next step. This is the perfect time to gain more knowledge. You

need to be highly careful while signing any deal or property papers this week. You can also be deceived or your faith and trust can be broken. Avoid spending your money on shares and debentures. You will get positive results, if you are awaiting any result. You will get justice and good outcomes.

Love
'Page of Swords' says that you can choose the wrong direction with your high power and zeal. You have to maintain the pace and move slowly after consulting your close ones for your personal matters.

Money
You are ready to enjoy the hard-earned money by working even harder. You will be continuously putting in the needed efforts. You will get positive outcomes.

Health
'The Sun' says that you will enjoy very good health this week.

Career
'Eight of Wands' says that you need to avoid the company of negative people otherwise; you can get influenced by their attitude. Follow your heart and move ahead.

Education
This is a highly prosperous time to enhance your

knowledge and gain valuable information from all directions.

Lucky numbers
3 and 5

Lucky colour
Magenta Pink

Lucky days
Monday, Wednesday and Saturday

Remedies
The environment and situation is likely to teach you a lesson. You need to learn and calculate the money you have gained. You are not getting much happiness in your personal life too. The reason behind this may be the money matters are not being handled properly. You have to do the needed by investing at the right areas. Yor can make a budget and follow it by curtailing unnecessary expenditures.

7th Week
(February 8 to 14)

Overview
'Queen of Swords' says that though you are analytical but you are not fully analyzing the situation whole-heartedly. You have to accept the positive and negative

sides of all situations. 'Four of Wands' says that you will be able to take up old job and finish them now in this week. You can even start new tasks this week. You will get success. 'The Star' says that you will be on a high, as all your wishes will be granted. You will get mental and emotional satisfaction. You will be very happy and you will even spread happiness and smile wherever you go this week. You need to be careful as this excitement and encouragement can lead you to the opposite way. You have to take utmost care and guidance from your well-wishers. They will show you the right path. 'The High Priestess' shows us that you are not fully utilizing your capabilities and energy. You are being idle, instead being more active by implementing your ideas and plans. You will face hard work and competition at the work place or at school. People are demanding and expecting more out of you and you need to fulfill their expectations so as to show your abilities. You need to be careful while helping people. People take your advantage. You will get support from your partner or spouse. Your emotional desires will be taken care of this weekend. Spend most of your time with your near ones.

Love

Singles may get proposals of offers. You will be on a high, as you will enjoy your personal life fully.

Money
You are ready to work for financial improvement of your status. You will get the positive results, as your efforts will be paid of.

Health
Health will be excellent as you are active through out the week.

Career
'Eight of Wands' indicates that you need to devote more time for education enhancement.

Education
You have to come out of the fixed idea and be more open and interactive. You shall mix and mingle with people who can help and give you valuable information.

Lucky numbers
2 and 7

Lucky colour
Saffron

Lucky days
Sunday, Monday and Saturday

Remedies
You may be involved in the wrong things this week. You have to maintain focus on your career and education. You need to try a new career line, as the

current career line is not of your interest. You can even pursue your hobbies as your career. You have to gain knowledge and implement it and this can be done by attending classes or lectures. You have to be dynamic and bold. Accept offers as they come to you.

8th Week
(Febuary 15 to 21)

Overview
'Seven of Pentacles' says that you will have to be on your toes and action oriented while dealing with money matters. You will be able to see inflow of money only if you invest it in the right direction. You are intelligent but use your intellect in analyzing the situation from both the sides. Then only you will get accurate results. You will get success in the current project and you can even start on the next task without wasting much time. You can even take up all the incomplete tasks and then finish them this week. You have to surrender yourself while undertaking a project. Spirituality will help you surpass the difficulties this week. Your colleagues are likely to give you a tough time at the work place by competing with you. You have to be cautious and take all the needed steps so as to win the race. Your hard work and patience will be tested this week. You need to

be cautious while working with others. You can be deceived or your trust can also be broken. Do not get dependent on others and do your work on your own. You have to prepare a list of priorities and take up the tasks one by one. This will help you tackling the tasks with perfection. At the end of the week, 'the Lovers' says that you can get romantic and spend most of your time with your life-partner. This will give you ease and also energize you for the coming week.

Love
You have to be highly careful with your words this week. You can hurt others if you try to be impulsive.

Money
You will be getting all the monetary benefits this week without any fail.

Health
'Nine of Cups' says that you can even take rest this week after a busy schedule. You can rejuvenate yourself this weekend. Health will be fine.

Career
You have to be interactive in an organization so as to work together. Exchange your ideas with others so that cooperation can be maintained.

Education
'Page of Cups' indicates that you will be highly

passionate and energetic this week regarding a new knowledgeable course.

Lucky numbers
5 and 6

Lucky colour
Turquoise Blue

Lucky days
Sunday, Monday and Saturday

Remedies
Do not trust any third person blindly this week or you can be deceived, so you have to be aware. You need not do anything out of the way for others and try to have a control by not being impulsive. You need stability in life. You can place a metal statue of God at home, as it will help and give you positive energy and blessings. You will be more active and vibrantly cheerful. You should be more interactive and this will enhance your public image.

9th Week
(February 22 to 28)

Overview
'Justice' says that you will get positive outcomes from areas where you have invested time, money and energy.

You will be satisfied with the results. After the results, you will be ready for more hard work and you will put in sincere efforts. The money, which you have earned through your hard work, needs to be invested in proper areas so that you do not get possessive regarding your wealth. 'Ace of Wands' says that this is the perfect time in order to upgrade your knowledge by acquiring information from all directions. You will get all the pleasures at the work place too. You have the intellect and you are even implementing it in the right direction. You will get the desired work and will be satisfied with the progress. You have to be interactive and expressive so that you do not create hurdles for yourself. You should take maximum advantage of the situations so as to keep the progress going on. 'The Magician' indicates that you will be admired and respected wherever you go. You spread smiles and happiness everywhere. You will be happy and content with the response you get form people. You can even go for social events. 'Ace of Swords' says that you will be the winner and at the top of the world this week. You will accomplish all your targets on time and this will be highly rewarding.

Love

'The Hermit' says that you can experience a sad phase as you are unable to devote time to your loved ones. Devote and spend more time with your close ones and do not give them any scope of complaint.

Money
You can get egoistic and possessive regarding your wealth this week. Be grounded and positive. Share your gains with others too.

Health
You will be enjoying good health this week but you have to be more responsive and use all the elements, which are in front of you.

Career
You will be at a top position where your juniors will seek your guidance and support.

Education
'The Temperance' says that you will be able to devote time to your individual upgradation this week. There is focus and you are determined.

Lucky numbers
1 and 3

Lucky colour
Red

Lucky days
Tuesday, Friday and Saturday

Remedies
You have to keep a control on your ego and doubting nature. You have to be dynamic. You can help your

juniors by teaching those new ways of learning and doing their work. You have always been a giver and now is a time when you have to accept the suggestions from other too. Project yourself in a way that others do have an influence on you. This will help you change your life and you will perceive situations from a better and positive outlook at the workplace and at home too.

10th Week
(March 1 to 7)

Overview

Initially you are likely to get offers and money from many sources and you will have to grab the best option without delay. You are speeding towards your destination. You have to slow down so that you do not take wrong decisions during this week. Be patient and steady. You can experience a time when you are unable to understand the situations that you face. You can even be indecisive. But during this time, you need to have faith in God by being spiritual and honest. You will get the path yourself. You will see things taking a 360° turn and you will be able to perceive the situations in a positive manner. You are likely to get showy and proud of your financial and material status. You can even go for some shopping and spending some money on yourself and your family members. 'Ten of Cups' says that you will be highly enjoying the time with your family and friends. You can even plan a reunion or a meeting with your close ones so that you get a sense of satisfaction and happiness. You will be highly gaining during the end of the week. You will share this success with others. You can receive money if stuck from a source. You will be highly energetic and cheerful rearing to take up new tasks. This is the perfect time to take up your hobbies and work on them.

Love

You will be highly satisfied with the progress of your love life. You will satisfy the needs of your partner and in return you are likely to get a positive response.

Money

'The Tower' says that you can suffer a setback just in case you plan to make any investment in shares or debentures. Beware of the decisions you take this week.

Health

'Judgment' says that you will enjoy good health as you are moving towards spiritualism and you will have the blessings of God.

Career

'Nine of Pentacles' says that you will be able to impress your boss this week with the help of your creativity and imagination.

Education
You will be highly interested in upgrading your education this week. You will be groomed overall as an individual too.

Lucky numbers
2 and 9

Lucky colour
Chocolate Brown

Lucky days
Thursday, Friday and Saturday

Remedies
You can feed your pet or someone's pet or any stray dog. Do not keep thinking about yourself and your money. Your attitude will change as you will have a sense of responsibility. Everything will be fine and you will be more content.

11th Week
(March 8 to 14)

Overview
'The World' indicates that the week starts on an amazing note giving you all pleasure and blessings this week. You will be undergoing an emotional flow but you may not want to express it. You shall rather be

expressive by advertising and projecting your feelings in the right way. You will be highly authoritative and powerful as far as your financial position is concerned. But you should help some needy rather than showing of your status. You will be more respected if you are in a position where you can help anybody. Be diplomatic and tactful so as to tackle any difficulties. 'Five of Cups' say that you need to get out of your past so that you are able to concentrate on your present and work accordingly. You should be happy that you haven't lost anything! You will get over the turmoil and look up to the expectations. You will enjoy the later half of this week. You will be analytical and evaluative as you will not want to repeat any mistakes. 'Knight of Wands' shows you that you are on the correct path and you will achieve success in every undertaking.

Love
You shall notice that your love life is being stagnant. The reason behind this stagnation can be that you are unable to satisfy the needs of your close ones.

Money
You will be able to have a smooth flow of money and material gains this week.

Health
'The Devil' says that your health can be a matter of

concern this week. You have to take utmost care of your well being.

Career
You will get the desired incentives this week. You are likely to get an increment or promotion which will even affect your financial position.

Education
You have to open up this week and accept the information or guidance you get from others.

Lucky numbers
1 and 8

Lucky colour
Green

Lucky days
Sunday, Thursday and Saturday

Remedies
You have to take out time for your relationships and health this week. You shall get influenced by other's ideas and suggestions. You can join yoga or exercise classes and follow a diet schedule. Also include green leafy vegetables in your diet this week. This will help you maintain your health and it will have a positive effect on your relations too.

12th Week
(March 15 to 21)

Overview

'The High Priestess' shows us that being highly intelligent and a creative person, you are not being active and wasting all your energy by being idle. You need to put all your energy to an effective use so that you can yield the maximum positive results. You may prove as a helping hand to your juniors this week. But you have to target your aims first and then look after their needs. You will be much happier if once you complete your tasks. You will be aiming higher as you have the vision, potential and creativity. You should stick to one plan and move ahead. 'The Star' says that you will be a cheerful and a vivacious person whom people will look up to. You will change the atmosphere and will make it more lovable. People will love and respect you. You may get emotional but you will be focused. This is the right time to express your feelings to someone special. 'Four of Cups' suggests that you can ignore and neglect the offers that are coming your way. You have to wake up and be more responsive and accept the best offer, and then only you will get the success if you utilize your opportunities well. You need to act as a more mature person while taking decisions and tackling various situations. You will be highly enthusiastic this week.

Love
You need to respect other's feelings so as to get the positive vibrations from them. Be more serious and respectful.

Money
'Ten of Wands' says that you can over-pressurize yourself this week by handling too many contracts or deals at the same time. Give others their share of responsibility too.

Health
You will get a helping hand this week. This person will have an influential role to play and thus you will be good in health.

Career
'Three of Cups' suggests that you will be enjoying your work as it gives you pleasure. You will even get the support of your staff and colleagues at the right time. You can even celebrate a recent victory.

Education
This week, rather than enhancing your own education, you will be helping others in upgrading their knowledge. You will see happiness and contentment in other's face.

Lucky numbers
2 and 3

Lucky colour
Pink

Lucky days
Monday, Tuesday and Wednesday

Remedies
You have to be more serious in your personal relationships and handle situations in a more organized way. You can keep Pink quartz with yourself as it enhances your personal image and relations. Give more attention to your life partner this week as they demand your presence. Light 5-7 Pink candles tied with a yellow ribbon everyday at home for five minutes. As the candle melts, you will also emotionally fall and melt for your loved one.

13th Week
(March 22 to 28)

Overview
'Six of Swords' says that you can face some hindrance while starting a new project, but this is the time when you need to use your intellect and experiences. You will be able to reach the finish line on time if you are

determined and sincere. You can get negative but this is the week, when you need to be mind-oriented. You are getting too much emotional and this can hamper your individual growth. Be positive and do not trust people at once. You will be able to see the things from a better positive angle. Your efforts will be recognized and you will come out on top. 'Six of Cups' says that you will now be treating and teaching everyone from your intellect and your resources. People will seek your guidance as they love and respect you. You have everything in front of you but you just have to cut down the blind-fold and use these elements in your favour. 'The Wheel of Fortune' is asking you to work full-heartedly and with focus. You should not work on probability basis this attitude itself will not let you reach your goals. You are likely to get romantic and highly emotional. Singles can finish their search by meeting their soul mates. You will be delighted with response of your partner. Do not get influenced by the influence of other people's attitude. You have to be positive and make sure that your work doesn't get affected.

Love
'Knight of Wands' says that this is an excellent time to enhance your personal life. People looking for deeper commitment can go further to tie the knot.

Money
Money needs a lot of attention. You can take help from

a person who can manage your finances with honesty and faith.

Health
Health will be outstanding as you are getting all the pleasure and luxuries in your personal life.

Career
'The Hierophant' says that at the office you might be helping your juniors by providing them the information they need. Career-front is fine.

Education
You should not be so disciplined that you do not accept changes. You have to be open and accept and adapt to the situations as they come by learning from these situations.

Lucky numbers
1 and 7

Lucky colour
Forest Green

Lucky days
Monday, Tuesday and Friday

Remedies
You are not spending properly in this week at the needed areas and this is because, you are not holding the work with proper mind and thought balance. Give time to money this week. Situations can worsen if not

attended properly and on time. You have to hold the things in a right manner.

14th Week
(March 29 to April 4)

Overview

'Ten of Swords' says that someone may break your trust and faith this week. Be highly careful while dealing with new people. You have to be more adaptable to the environment. You need not cut down from the environment that is around you. Be free and open to the people you trust the most. You can face competition at the work place and this time, you will have to put in all the efforts sincerely without thinking about the results. Your hard work will be paid of on time. You may notice that you are not getting the desired results despite all efforts, and the reason behind this may be that you are working whole-heartedly. Invest at the right time, so that you do not regret at the last minute. 'The Temperance' says that your focus and balance will help you reap all the gains. This is a highly prosperous time to start on new projects. 'The Wheel of Fortune' shows us that the new projects need your full devotion and sincerity. You have to work full-heartedly and not on probability basis. You will get accurate results. 'Eight of Wands' says that you shall not get influenced by the influence of other people. You have to stay positive and be determined and stick to one plan. 'The Lovers' says that you can get passionate towards a particular person at the end of this week. You will get the much-needed support from this person.

Love
Relations need a lot of attention this week. You can get possessive about a person, but you have to give space and time to all your relations.

Money
You will get lots of financial benefits this week and you need to make the needed investments so as to move ahead.

Health
'Page of Pentacles' says that you are lively and cheerful this week, which helps you keep happy and on your toes. Your health will be fine.

Career
'The Sun' says that your career is now going to blossom and bloom. You will get the results that you are expecting by puting the needed efforts on time.

Education
Education will take a further step and you can even go on fulfilling your hobbies this week.

Lucky numbers
1 and 5

Lucky colour
Maroon

Lucky days
Wednesday, Thursday and Saturday

Remedies
You are getting negative this week, so in the morning, stand in front of the mirror and repeat three times, that "I am happy and satisfied", for 40 days. You will not get affected due to the negative attitude of people. Your tolerance power will improve and you also need to share your feelings and thoughts with people.

15th Week
(April 5 to 11)

Overview
'Page of Wands' says that you will be highly energetic and cheerful. You are full of enthusiasm and this attitude will attract people and you are likely to get work of your own choice. You should not try your hand at every offer, as this will lack perfection. You need to hit the target and work with perfection. 'Four of Wands' says that you will see all your pending work getting completed on time. This is the perfect time to initiate new work as your energy and enthusiasm will help you reap better projects. Surrender yourself to the task

that you take up. A particular persona may also demand your attention this week. 'The World' says that you will be blessed and taken care of with the help of all the divine powers. This will give you a push and you will work even more. You can notice a change in the atmosphere and surroundings. This change can be even before your betterment and improvement. You have to stay determined and positive. There is likely to be a revolution and total transformation. 'Judgment' says that students who are awaiting results will get positive news and you will be satisfied with the outcome. You have God's blessings and things will turn out in your favour. You will be happier with the results and this will call for a celebration. People will now know you for the work you have accomplished.

Love
You will be guiding others, but you also need to accept changes from others.

Money
You will see new heights this week in your financial status. You will be content and satisfied.

Health
'The Star' says that health will be fantastic this week. You will not face any problem or hindrance from your health.

Career

'Ace of Pentacles' says that your career is at the top in the list of your priorities. You will even prove your capabilities and potential.

Education

'Ace of Cups' says that though your mind is on your relations and career, you will take out time for your personal enhancement this week.

Lucky numbers

4 and 5

Lucky colour

Lilac

Lucky days

Monday, Wednesday and Saturday

Remedies

You are not serious regarding the management of money. Money is a very important and an effective part of our life which has to be taken care of. Do not behave in an immature way. You can place Chinese coins in the south east direction wrapped in Red cloth or tied in a Red thread. This will help you to bring stability and prosperity and that in turn will increase you financial status.

16th Week
(April 12 to 18)

Overview

'Knight of Cups' says that you are focused and determined as far as your emotions and aims are concerned. You will get the desired results. You are ready to face the hard work and work accordingly towards the achievement of your goals. You will have lots of gains financially, materially and personally. You were looking forward to this gain and now is the time to enjoy the gains and benefits. You can guide others, only when they need your support. Do not waste your energy unnecessarily. You can face disappointment. You have to remove the grid inside which you are curbing yourself. You have to be flexible and not rigid. You need to see the things from all angles instead of fixing your mind frame and ideas. 'Three of Pentacles' says that some one is likely to come for your help this week either at the workplace or at home. The person will have a positive impact on you. You can even receive stuck money. Do not trust anyone while making investment decisions this week as you can be deceived. There are indications of losses but you need to learn from your mistakes and move ahead forgetting the past concentrating on your future. You can plan a holiday trip this week, as there are indications of a journey and this is the perfect time to spend money and energy on your family.

Love
Open up and be expressive in your relations. If you do not express your thoughts, you can head towards a communication gap and people can misunderstand you.

Money
You will be enjoying your position and wealth this week. Help the needy and work for the betterment of yourself and your surroundings.

Health
'Queen of Wands' says that you will definitely get the needed resources and you will enjoy your health this week.

Career
You will be rearing to take up new work as it gives you pleasure. Your talent will be utilized in a right manner.

Education
'The Devil' says that you are neglecting your education this week, and this can hamper your personal growth and improvement.

Lucky numbers
4 and 7

Lucky colour
Yellow Mustard

Lucky days
Sunday, Monday and Saturday

Remedies
You are being materialistic and running after the pleasure which you get materially and monetarily. You have to concentrate on other aspects of life too. Try to help and satisfy the needs of other people by distributing your work load with them. You have to maintain good relations with your employers so as to impress them, do some charity work this week. Maintain your good behaviour and also your public relations.

17th Week
(April 19 to 25)

Overview
'King of Swords' says that you will be evaluating the situations deeply and this gives you positive hope for tomorrow and the stamina to face the difficulties that can come in your way. You have to move ahead by forgetting and leaving behind your past and bitter experiences. You will only be benefited when you think about your future and work in the present. You will get

positive rewards wherever you have invested time, money and energy. You will be satisfied with the outcomes. You can create obstacles in your path by doubting your own capabilities. You have to be mature and understand the fact that you have the power and the strength to face all the obstacles with courage and focus. You will surpass all these hindrances. 'King of Wands' indicates that you will want to move ahead with a positive force, and you will even achieve the target but you may face a dilemma or slow pace. You will be getting time to check all your gains. Be patient and enjoy all the fruits by sharing your gains with your family and friends. At the end of the week, you are likely to pay attention to your partner. You will get the support from your partner/spouse.

Love
You will be benefited in your personal life this week as you get the support and you may even see that some one is taking interest in you.

Money
'King of Pentacles' says that, you can get possessive and selfish regarding money matters. Distribute the gains among your family members and move ahead while keeping your feet on the ground.

Health
Health will be perfect this week, as you are active and in this way, you are not risking your health.

Career
'The Tower' says that sacrifices can cause a downfall from your position. Do not sacrifice any more, rather complete your work first before starting the work for some one else.

Education
You are unable to concentrate on your education this week, may be because you are pre occupied. Education has no end, so take out time for your knowledge enhancement.

Lucky numbers
2 and 6

Lucky colour
Aqua Marine

Lucky days
Monday, Friday and Saturday

Remedies
You can wear an Eight mukhi Ganesh Rudraksh. Do not trust people without evaluating them. The Rudraksh will help you avoid all difficulties and obstacles on time. You will be able to maintain your

focus on your career. You need to write on a White sheet of paper that your career is on the right track and you are yielding lot of benefits. Keep this application near God's statue and read it three times every day for a week, and you will see a big change in your life.

18th Week
(April 26 to May 2)

Overview

'Ten of Cups' says that you kick start this week with an amazing zeal as you get the much needed support from people you love. You have to use all your capabilities up to the mark without wasting your talent and intellect. You can get detached with the environment, but that's not the solution to a problem. You have to devote time and think patiently while facing a difficulty. You will be back on the track as you are now cheerful and excited about the new ventures that are likely to come your way. 'Ace of Swords' suggests that you will be on top as the king and you see all your dreams fulfilling this week making you the winner. People will be praising and admiring you all the way. Now that you have accomplished your goals, for post work services, you may have to do some manipulations or be diplomatic. Then only you seem to have some hope for positive results. Do not get over-excited, the route can get diverted. This is the time when you have to plan and exchange thoughts with your elders and correct your mistakes.

Love
Though you get the support, you should not pressurize yourself with additional burden. Give time to everyone and then come to a fair decision. Personal life needs lot of attention.

Money
Money prospects are looking bright this week. You just have to use your environment for more enhancement of your monetary position.

Health
'The Empress' says that you will be content while guiding others. Health will not trouble you this week as you are taking up the activity of your own choice.

Career
Career can take a wrong direction if you neglect the right offers and overload yourself. Take advice from others before implementing your own ideas.

Education
Be more action oriented rather than evaluating the terms and conditions. You have to be on your toes and accept the changes in your surroundings.

CAPRICORN

Lucky numbers
7 and 8

Lucky colour
Sea Green

Lucky days
Sunday, Wednesday and Thursday

Remedies
Set your tasks and your priorities on time. You need to use Yellow colour this week so as to enhance your courage by including Yellow fruits in your diet. This will give you clarity of thought. Distribute Yellow fruits among children and everything will fall in place.

19th Week
(May 3 to 9)

Overview
The week starts on a high note when you are enjoying and celebrating your victory. You are taking some time off and you will definitely get ease and pleasure. Do not be indecisive while taking decisions. Be down to earth and have faith in God, he will surely show you the path, but you just have to take the initiative. 'The Moon' suggests that you doubt others, do not doubt. You can even get egoistic with this attitude. This can become a

hindrance on your path too. Invest at the right areas so as to yield maximum returns. You have to be practical and more courageous while making such decisions. 'Queen of Swords' says that though you are analytical, you are not using your intellect in the right direction. Evaluate the situation on the whole so as to have a better and a clearer view of the situations. You will get busy while helping others with their work. You have to pamper yourself this week-end by going to the spa or getting rejuvenated by taking on your hobbies. You will be the centre of attraction wherever you go this week. Social events can be fruitful and beneficial if you attend and mingle with people. You are likely to get spiritual and you can devote sometime by praying or focusing more on your aims.

Love
You will get the needed atmosphere where you get to meet people of your choice. This is a highly prosperous time to enhance and initiate new relations.

Money
'Queen of Pentacles' says that you will earn lot of gains but you need not get showy. You can plan shopping this week.

Health
'Six of Cups' says that you are a giver and you will take care of the needs of other people this week. This attitude

will give you ease and relaxation. You will enjoy good health.

Career
You have to be analytical and not emotional while considering your career. You have to be bold and courageous this week at the work place.

Education
You will be ready to upgrade your education level by taking active participation wherever you go.

Lucky numbers
3 and 9

Lucky colour
Green

Lucky days
Tuesday, Wednesday and Friday

Remedies
There is doubt in your career and in this way, you are unable to decide. Do take advice from others but do not get dependent on them. Feed the birds early morning as it will help you finish all your tasks well within time.

20th Week
(May 10 to 16)

Overview
'Six of Cups' says that you are a giver and you will take care of the needs of other people this week. Your giving nature will continue for some time and you will derive pleasure and satisfaction from this attitude. A third persona is likely to come to your help and this person will be beneficial to you either at the home or at office. You can plan an outing with your family this week by taking a break from your work. You have to make arrangements and take investment decisions. Do not opt for shortcuts this week like spending money in shares or debentures. You can be deceived if you blindly trust some one. Do not get emotional, instead use your intellect and take practical decisions. 'Nine of Cups' says that you will now be evaluating and enjoying the fruits of the hard work done. You will come out on top with your creative and imaginative abilities.

Love
'Six of wands' says that you will be highly happy and content with your personal life as all your needs will be satisfied this week.

Money
'The Lover' says that you are likely to get passionate towards your gains. Enjoy but do not get egoistic.

Health
'Two of Wands' says that you are very well-maintained and your health will support you in every sphere.

Career
'King of Wands' says that you will be satisfied with the current position. You are likely to implement new plans but it will take time.

Education
You will be highly interested in learning new things as they come by you.

Lucky numbers
1 and 6

Lucky colour
Golden Yellow

Lucky days
Sunday, Tuesday and Saturday

Remedies
You want name, fame and positive results. You will get surety and security while working efficiently. You have to maintain this position in the future too and this can be done by behaving nicely and positively with everyone. Carry a Red pen or a Red flower with yourself as it will give you the much needed energy and enthusiasm.

21st Week
(May 17 to 23)

Overview

You are vivacious and you give a colour wherever you go. Everyone enjoy the atmosphere when you are around. You are able to strike a balance between your personal and professional life, but you have to avoid ego. You have God's blessing and move ahead with hope and positive attitude. (Your advantage can be taken, and this situation can lead to indecisiveness. You have to be more practical and calm while facing any difficulty. God will shower his blessings on you and you will definitely find a way out. Now that you are out of the difficult phase, you need to realize that you are full of resources and elements that you need. Make full utilization of these things in your favour. Do not be over impulsive, while taking decisions. Your high level of enthusiasm can lead you to the opposite way and you can be in trouble. Consult your elders this week. You will rise out of all the difficult situations as a winner and will shine as bright as the sun. Do not get possessive and egoistic while evaluating your gains and income. Keep your feet on ground and take the next step after examination and scrutinizing the situation well.

Love
'The Moon' suggests that you can become egoistic and this can hamper your relations with your loved ones. Be patient and not impulsive. Your close ones need your time and energy.

Money
You need to be manipulative and diplomatic while dealing in financial matters, as it will help you gain more income.

Health
Health will be fine this week as your energy and liveliness is being utilized fully.

Career
'Page of Pentacles' indicates that you have to be mature and more cautious though you are full of life and energy. Take advice from your elders this week.

Education
You are fast to learn new things. Do not neglect your environment and surroundings. Be steady and accept the changes as they come.

Lucky numbers
1 and 9

Lucky colour
White

Lucky days
Sunday, Monday and Friday

Remedies
You should believe in yourself and in your abilities. Boost your self-confidence from time to time by not being disappointed. There is a need to evaluate and calculate each step and every movement so as to maintain the self confidence and strength. You have to remove the feeling of insecurity from inside by being courageous. Enhance your environment with Orange colour as it will help you being more ambitious. Use Orange colour by means of including it in your dressing style, or using semi precious or precious stones. You can even wear a Carnelian necklace so as to enhance your courage.

22nd Week
(May 24 to 30)

Overview
'King of Cups' says that though you are being emotional you are not expressive and reactive. Do not be cold to emotions. This week you may have to be straight-forward and open with your thoughts. Do not get so emotional that others have a say on you. You should not get influenced by others rather be influential. 'Ace of Wands' says that you will be able to establish and

accomplish all your goals on time. You will want to gain more knowledge and you will be sucreeded in your ambitions. You are highly analytical and evaluative. This will help you understand future situations and give you hope for future. You will get justice in all the legal matters and you will get positive response if awaiting any judgment. There is a need to forget the past and move ahead with a positive attitude for fulfilling all your dreams and aim. Be happy with what you are holding in hand. 'Four of Pentacles' says that you are likely to fix your ideas and thoughts. You shall not be rigid, as it can have a negative impact on your behaviour. 'Eight of Swords' says that you have to be open instead of cutting yourself from your environment. Be expressive and clear in your thoughts and expression. Avoid communication gap.

Love
Though you have everything in front of you, you are not action-oriented instead evaluating the characters you meet. Be responsive and according to the situations.

Money
'The Chariot' says that money will flow in smoothly and you will be satisfied.

Health
Health will be supportive and you will enjoy high level of energy this week.

Career
You are ready to face the competition with determination, stable mind and hard work.

Education
'Death Card' reveals that there is a reversal of situation for your betterment and you will make full utilization of these situations.

Lucky numbers
4 and 7

Lucky colour
Peacock Blue

Lucky days
Monday, Tuesday and Wednesday

Remedies
There are lot of movement this week. You have to explore new transaction and events this week. There will be smooth changes in your life. Energy and excitement will bring in new developments for you. Have faith in god and carry yourself in a disciplined way. Keep your mentor's picture with yourself so as to avoid unwanted tension.

23rd Week
(May 31 to June 6)

Overview

'The Magician' says that you are going to attract the people around you. They will like your cheerful nature as you spread happiness and smile among them. Do not overload yourself with all the responsibilities at one time. Be patient as you have enough time to tackle these tasks one by one. Each and every task has to be completed with perfection. 'Three of Cups' says that this is the time when you can have a blast and enjoy with your friends and family. This is the time when you can celebrate and enjoy social events. Enjoy your financial position by spending a part of income on yourself. Do not get showy instead support people with your monetary status when needed. 'Eight of Cups' says that now you are likely to detach yourself from your environment. This is not a good indication as the people around you will support you when you need them the most. Due to detachment you may feel that things are getting stagnant and not moving at the pace you expected. The reason behind this can be your negligence and your half-heartedness. Work with full dedication. You are likely to create obstacles by yourself if you do not change your attitude. Analyze the situation from both the positive and negative aspects so as to yield maximum returns.

Love
You are ready for a deeper commitment and you will succeed in your ambitions.

Money
You are now aiming high and ready to take up challenges and manage your finances in a positive and better way.

Health
You are likely to overload yourself and this will have a negative impact on your health. Health needs care this week.

Career
'The Hanged Man' says that career prospects will be better only when there is clarity in your thought process.

Education
Accept the situation as they are and work full-heartedly to attain more knowledge about your surroundings.

Lucky numbers
1 and 3

Lucky colour
Pink

Lucky days
Monday, Tuesday and Saturday

Remedies
You are having extra zeal and energy, use this energy in a positive way by balancing your act. Do not think that you only can do everything and do not overload yourself. Give others a chance too. You are also being critical and your ego can even hurt you. You have to surrender yourself and enhance your IQ level. Practice meditation or listen to slow and soothing music everyday for 30 minutes with your eyes closed.

24th Week
(June 7 to 13)

Overview
You are focused and emotional and know the path that you have undertaken. You will achieve your aim if you go on with the same level of determination. You have the mind and thoughts which you are now implementing in the right direction. You can face high competition but just be focused. You need to prove your worth and this is the right time to do it. 'Ace of Pentacles' suggests that this is the perfect time to make investments in property and shares too. You will be highly benefited from these investments and rolling of money. You shall

not get possessive and show off your position to others; this shows your negative traits too. Be grounded and help the needy at the right time. You will earn respect. Surrender yourself and try to concentrate on your task, some at a time. You may have to sacrifice some pleasure of life but it surely will give future benefits. Use all your energy, capabilities and potentials now so as to benefit and yield maximum benefits.

Love
You are going to be over responsible. Devote time and space on time. You will be benefited this way. Be calm and patient.

Money
'The Emperor' indicates that you may be guiding and taking care of other people and their finances. You have to take care of your monetary position and then divert your energy toward others.

Health
'Four of Cups' says that health is a matter of concern this week. You have to take care even if you are struck with minor ailments.

Career
'Two of Cups' says that you will be highly drawn towards your work and tasks. You will work with full focus and dedication.

Education
You have to be highly careful while experiencing new situations. Learn maximum from whatever you experience.

Lucky numbers
2 and 4

Lucky colour
Green

Lucky days
Sunday, Tuesday and Saturday

Remedies
You are being over-loaded with lot of responsibilities and tasks. You have to distribute and share these tasks with others too. You have to reach your targets on time, so be organized and planned. You are neither accepting which can lead to unhappiness. You are holding things in a wrong way which needs to be corrected. Use more of Green colour in your daily routine. You can even plant a tree in the north-east direction. Bamboo plant can be bought or gifted to someone as it would be perfect in order to enhance your education. There will be a flow of energy and power

25th Week
(June 14 to 20)

Overview
You will be highly satisfied with your financial status. You are likely to help others by providing them monetary support. You can face some initial difficulties but you will definitely surpass them with the help of your tact and experience. 'Two of Pentacles' says that you may receive and even let go some offers and money in hope for even better offers. You have to opt for the best opportunity and start working upon it right away. Do not get influenced by other's attitude. Be individualistic and firm. 'The Devil' suggests that you can get highly motivated and highly interested in a particular task or a person. Do not get hyper or impatient, it can lead you to a wrong way. You will have the blessings from God and you will definitely be benefited from your work and efforts. 'Ace of Cups' says that you will get emotional and sentimental this week diverting all your energy towards your partner. This is the time when singles can get committed. Use all your capabilities in a right manner and be more action oriented this week.

Love
you may not be very happy with your love life, the reason may be that you are not giving time and space to your

relations. Give others to express their views and ideas.

Money
Money prospects are looking highly bright for you. Enjoy all the incentives and benefits.

Health
'Six of Cups' says that giving and helping others gives you ease and pleasure. This will keep you happy and you will even enjoy your health.

Career
'King of Wands' says that you are trying to implement new ideas and your imagination, but you may find yourself stagnant. This stagnation is temporary; your flight will take-of soon. Be patient.

Education
You will be willing and interested in learning new things. Use your wit and intellect to know better and positive things about your surroundings.

Lucky numbers
6 and 9

Lucky colour
Almond Brown

Lucky days
Monday, Thursday and Friday

Remedies

Do not give much importance to people who do not respect your guidance. You need to read all the terms and conditions before you sign any deal or contract as you can be deceived if you are negligent. Take blessings from God and from your elders especially. You can even place a Crystal quartz' or Shree-yantra at your office desk. This will give you stability and strength.

26th Week
(June 21 to 27)

Overview

'Knight of Cups' says that you will be focused and moving forward steadily analyzing the situations. You will be emotional too. You will be focusing all your energy towards your partner or spouse. Do not get dependent or do not get over involved. You will notice things around you will take a turn and some situations can even worsen. You have to be highly practical and positive so as to yield maximum gains from such situations. Do not doubt at the first place before implementing your plans. This itself will not be beneficial if you start working on probability basis. 'The Strength' says that you will have to be diplomatic this week. People will see your other side and this can be beneficial in some difficult situations. 'The Fool' says that your cheerful and carefree nature will help you attract people towards you. You can get spiritual this week. Be careful and serious while handling finances. You will see yourself on the top. People will see you as an influential individual. You will be positive having an impact on your surroundings.

Love
'Queen of Swords' says that you are being one sided in your relations which will not do you any good. You have to give space and time to your close ones so as to get positive response.

Money
'Ace of Swords' says that you will be the ultimate winner as far as your money matters are seen. You will manage your finances very well this week.

Health
Your health is very positive this week, giving you energy, enthusiasm and positivism

Career
'The Moon' says that you are likely to get egoistic regarding your position. Be grounded and keep working with the same frequency. Your ego can bring you down.

Education
You are speeding up to learn new things and take up

new ventures. Slow down as while speeding you may not be able to notice your surroundings and environment.

Lucky numbers
1 and 6

Lucky colour
Purple

Lucky days
Sunday, Wednesday and Saturday

Remedies
You are being one sided in your love life and financial status. You have to analyze both the positive and the negative aspects of life. Be firm in your decisions by keeping aside your ego and doubt. Spend your money wherever necessary. For extra zeal and energy you can take advice from your elders and seniors at the work place. You need to inform everybody about your plans so that you get suggestions from others.

27th Week
(June 28 to July 4)

Overview
'The Empress' indicates that this week, you will divert and devote all your energy while helping and satisfying

the needs of others. You will take care of the wants and needs of people who are around you. If students are waiting for any results this week, they are likely to secure positive results and good marks. You will be benefited monetarily and this will act as a boost to your energy level. You are likely to receive and let go money and some offers which come your way. A third person will come for your help. You can receive support and guidance from this third person either at your office or at home. You are likely to get stuck money back. This week is highly prosperous as far as your financial position is considered. Make investments at the right time, for future security. Though you are financially stable, you need to organize and implement your ideas by being action-oriented. Recognize the incentives and the benefits which are in front of you.

Love
You will be responsible for everyone's well being as you are ready to take the commitment and responsibility. New relations can be initiated.

Money
'Five of Wands' says that money matters need care as you are having excess of money. You have to take proper care by investing at the right time.

Health
'Page of Cups' says that your health will be excellent as you are mentally fit this week.

Career
'Seven of Wands' indicates that you are ready for the up-coming struggle. You will get fruitful results as you are putting in the right amount of efforts.

Education
Education prospects are looking very bright as you are ready to undertake new ventures.

Lucky numbers
3 and 6

Lucky colour
Green Forest

Lucky days
Sunday, Monday and Thursday

Remedies
You are showing immaturity. Though you have lots of money and there is prosperity, you need stability and you have to improve the ability to accept suggestions from others. You have to be determined and move ahead. You can keep a Pyramid on your office table or a globe. Keep a Crystal show-piece which will give you stability and negativity will not influence you.

28th Week
(July 5 to 11)

Overview
The moon suggests that you are likely to get egoistic and doubtful regarding your environment and the people around you. Be practical and move ahead with confidence. You will definitely see the things falling on your side. You will come out on top as the ultimate winner. You will then begin to look for more ventures by putting additional efforts. You will see an occasion to enjoy and celebrate. You are likely to receive good news from a relative. Do not get possessive with the gains as there is tendency being reflected. Be ready to share your gains with others. You are likely to start a new project by investing a lot of energy and sincere efforts. You will get success in this project. Make sure you have full knowledge regarding this venture before you implement your knowledge. Do not get negative by the influence of other people. Be mind-oriented and not heart-oriented. 'The Devil' suggests that you can get highly motivated in respect to this project or a person in particular. Do not depend on a single person; it can harm your aims and intentions.

Love
'Eight of Cups' says that you want to move away from all the emotional bondages. This can create a communication gap between you and your relatives.

You need to spend more time with your family this week.

Money
There is stagnation in your money department this week. The reason is that you are not ready to make a move and invest. In order to move forward you need to take the right steps.

Health
You have to keep away from people who have a negative influence on you. Health needs a lot of attention.

Career
'Page of Wands' indicates that you are highly enthusiastic and energetic this week, which keeps you away from mental tensions

Education
'The World' says that you will have many offers which would help you to enhance your education and knowledge this week. You have all the blessings to make a decision and move ahead.

Lucky numbers
3 and 8

Lucky colour
Lemon Yellow

Lucky days
Sunday, Tuesday and Thursday

Remedies

Your love life seems to get affected this week. Do not think negative as your mind is fixed this week. There is a balance needed and the balance can be achieved by distributing all the tasks and responsibilities with your mates and colleagues. You have to work in a positive environment this week. Take bath using salt water as it will diffuse all the negative vibrations from you. Also clean your surroundings with salt water. You are not supposed to self-doubt your capabilities and potential.

29th Week
(July 12 to 18)

Overview

'The Tower' says that the week is likely to start on a low note, as you are sacrificing a lot for your loved ones at home and colleagues at your office. You have to keep your confidence level high this week. After so much of sacrifices, you are likely to get highly emotional and sentimental. Do not be cold to emotions; rather express your feelings in a right manner to the right person. You will be benefited by this expression of love and concern. You are highly a focused person who has a confidence on his/her potentials. 'Queen of Wands' says that you will be enjoying a good position this week. People will come up to you and expect guidance and support from you. You have an authority and power which should not be misused. You will now aim higher and keep your focus intact. You are on the right track and you will get the expected results. 'Knight of Wands' indicates that you are full of life and enthusiasm. You will win-over many hearts and this leaves a good impression on other people. Your positive force will take you to places. Do not get dependent on a single person. Your emotional needs will be satisfied this week, as you will get the support from your partner/spouse. Do not show off your monetary position, as it can hamper your status.

Love
You are likely to start on with a new relation with someone close. You are likely to be highly satisfied and impressed.

Money
You can get possessive this week which can even lead to a communication gap. Be ready to help the needy and serve their needs.

Health
Health is a highly important matter of concern this week. Take care of your health even if you are infected by small infections.

Career
You have to be open and receptive to the suggestions of other people. Interaction with colleagues will be of much use.

Education
Education is unable to get time as your mind is busy and tensed. Take out time for your self up gradation this week.

Lucky numbers
1 and 9

Lucky colour
Red

Lucky days
Monday, Tuesday and Friday

Remedies
You are wasting all your energy while sacrificing and helping others. Do not try to be over-protective and highly concerning. Give time and space to all your relationships. This will also help you maintain good health. Check out your diet schedule. You can even go to the doctor for an overall check up this week. There is everything available in front of you but still there is a hindrance in your career. Take out time for yourself as there is an overall balance needed.

30th Week
(July 19 to 25)

Overview
In the beginning of the week itself, you seem to have some manipulations and diplomacy so as to move head

with full confidence. You will be busy helping and guiding others with their work. You are likely to use your intellect and mind while helping others. People will be seeking your help and support. You will get justice in all the work and tasks that you take up this week. All legal matters will be cleared with positive outcomes. Be frank and free while exchanging your views and thoughts with others. Do not try to hide or be aloof. You should be among people so that they also get to know about your ideas. You will surely come out on top as a persona who has the willingness and the power to work. You will get all the benefits that you need plus the love and support from your close ones. 'Nine of Cups' says that this week, you will be enjoying the fruits of your success and gains. You will be content and happy with the way your life is progressing. After so much of enjoyment and celebration, you are likely to work on probability basis, by putting in efforts half-heartedly. You shall not think about the results in the beginning, just do your work and leave the rest on God.

Love
'Seven of Swords' says that you are likely to take up many things at a time regarding your relations. You have to be specific and give time individually to your relations.

Money
'Queen of Swords' says that you are not using your intellect in a right manner. Use all your experiences

and take guidance from your elders while taking decisions regarding money matters.

Health
Health needs a lot of attention. Consult the doctor before you take up any medication.

Career
You have to move ahead forgetting the past failures. It can have a demoralizing effect on you.

Education
You shall take up the opportunities that you are seeing in front of you. You will be able to move ahead if you take up that initiative willingly.

Lucky numbers
2 and 8

Lucky colour
Lilac

Lucky days
Sunday, Monday, Wednesday

Remedies
There is a need to change of place this week, and this can be done by planning a holiday trip with your family. Take a break from the routine life and enjoy some time for yourself. Rejuvenate yourself and charge your battery by going out and enjoying.

31st Week
(26 July to August 1)

Overview

'Eight of Swords' says that the week begins with slight confusion as you are not open and free to your loved ones. Be responsive and tactful while talking and expressing your feelings. You have to be decisive and firm in your decisions this week. Take help if needed from your elders. You are likely to go on a trip this week, which will have an influential affect on you. Take full advantage of this trip and you will see more offers coming your way. You can even plan a holiday trip with your family this weekend. You can face small initial hurdles which might divert your attention, but your experience will prove handy in this case. You will be able to surpass these obstacles successfully. In this way, you are likely to overload your self with extra responsibilities this week. Do not get stressed up by over-pressurizing yourself. You need to share these responsibilities with your colleagues and complete one task at a time. You have to be more focused in terms of your concentration and dedication towards your work. This can be done by totally surrendering and getting engrossed in your work. 'Knight of Cups' says that this will be a time when you can to strike a balance between your emotions while keeping your focus on your work too. You will be getting satisfaction with the way you work this week. Do not doubt your capabilities and potentials. This can be harmful for your venture. You need to have full confidence and move ahead without fear.

Love
'Two of Wands' says that you will be content with your personal life as you are able to take out time for your family.

Money
Money prospects are looking highly bright and prosperous this week. Make the needed arrangements so as to make your future secure.

Health
Health will be perfect this week. Enjoy the week to the fullest without over loading yourself.

Career
'Five of Swords' says that at the career front, you will be unable to focus on one task as you are trying to tackle all the tasks at a time. Be more specific and take up the tasks one at a time.

Education
You are highly satisfied with the improvement which you are showing in your education enhancement. You shall not stop instead move forward as you are the strength and power.

Lucky numbers
4 and 7

Lucky colour
Silver Grey

Lucky days
Monday, Wednesday and Friday

Remedies
Do not try any shortcuts in career, you can suffer losses. You are taking things in a very fast manner. Analyze your steps and actions before implementing them for a long term benefit. Prioritize your tasks and then write it on a sheet of paper and complete your work on time. Analyze your performance at the end of the day. This will help you finish your tasks according to your talents and capabilities.

32nd Week
(August 2 to 8)

Overview
'Two of Cups' says that this week starts on a highly romantic and emotional note. This is a very bright week, when singles can meet someone new who has an influence on you. You may be sad or depressed as you can be showing light and guidance to people who do not need or respect your suggestions. You have to keep your experience with yourself so that you can take full

advantage of it sometime later. You have the experience which you need to put in use when needed. You will excel in your undertaking. 'Seven of Pentacles' says that you have to be more action oriented rather than counting and evaluating your gains and income. Be more active and take needful steps so as to invest you money for future purposes. 'The Fool' shows us that you will be carefree and cheerful this week and as a result you can even impress your seniors or colleagues. You have to see the pros and cons before taking any strong step. You will be glad as you will take out time for your family and fulfill their expectations. Your family and friends will be happy and satisfied with your presence. 'Six of Wands' says that this will be highly prosperous time when people will get to know you more. You will be all over the places as you have proven your capabilities. Social events are likely to take place this week, where you will be the centre of discussion. Now that you have achieved your goals, you may try and help people who need guidance. But make sure that you do not spend all your energy in helping and supporting others, as your health can get affected.

Love
'Page of Wands' says that you will be highly enthusiastic about a recent change in your personal life. You are looking forward to more enthusiasm.

Money
Finances need a lot of care as there is a sudden loss

being indicated this week. You have to be highly careful while signing any important deals.

Health
'Four of Pentacles' says that you are in a set mind frame which is not allowing you to fully focus and consider your health. Health needs care this week if attitude doesn't change.

Career
You are taking the steps after deep analysis and with practicality. You will take meaningful steps and you will succeed without fail.

Education
'The Sun' says that at the education front, you will be of immense importance to others. You will shine as the Sun and maintain the dignity.

Lucky numbers
1 and 9

Lucky colour
Saffron

Lucky days
Monday, Thursday and Friday

Remedies
Do not be materialistic. You have to forgive and be happy with the people around you. You can suffer sudden losses. Invest at the right time in the right areas, which give you maximum benefits. You can keep a Silver coin

with yourself or a currency symbol and pray to God that you get financial security and surety in the future.

33rd Week
(August 9 to 15)

Overview
'Ten of Cups' indicates that this week, you will be family oriented and enjoying time with your friends and loved ones. This will give you rest and pleasure. You can get indecisive regarding your career as your main focus is on family and personal life. You need to take out time for your professional life too. A person at the office is likely to take undue advantage of you. Be careful while revealing important data. You will be back to your normal self as soon as people around you will start enjoying your company. You will bring happiness and smiles wherever you go. 'The Wheel of Fortune' says that you may work on doubtful and hit and trial basis without working whole-heartedly. You need to put in efforts with full dedication so as to earn good results. You will earn lot of financial and material gains. You will be on cloud nine after this success. 'Seven of Swords' says that after so much of gains you can get deviated from your path and take up unnecessary tasks which can have a negative effect on you. You will be speeding to go and reach your targets. You need to move steadily at a slower pace because slow and steady wins the race.

Love
You will want to take a step forward towards commitment this week. You are likely to get positive response.

Money
You are planning to help others this week with their finances. People around you will be seeking and appreciating your help.

Health
'The Strength' says that you can face minor ailments this week. Do not neglect any small infection or ailment as it can take a major shape.

Career
'Eight of Swords' says that you have to mingle with your surroundings so as to get meaningful and important information.

Education
You have to surrender yourself to the changes and adapt them as you come across. This will help you enhance and upgrade your education.

Lucky numbers
1 and 8

Lucky colour
Aqua Marine

Lucky days
Tuesday, Thursday and Friday

Remedies

You need to listen any spiritual channel or bhajans which have a soothing effect on your mind and soul. Stand in front of God with your hands joined and pray for your wellbeing. You have to surrender yourself to the almighty so as to get happiness

34th Week
(August 16 to 22)

Overview

'The Hermit' says that you are likely to depress this week as the ones whom you are trying to help will not be keen in taking your advice. You have to be more specific while helping and guiding others. Your helping hand will continue guiding others for sometime this week. You have to be careful as someone can take advantage of you in this way. 'Six of Pentacles' says that you will be elated with the gains that come your way. This will act as a positive boost for you and you will take more pride in your work. You need to implement your plans as then only your capabilities will be recognized and you will get the much needed appraisal. Your plans and thoughts need to be worked upon as being idle will not work for you in a positive way. 'Nine of Cups' says that your will be encouraged as you will be evaluating and enjoying your gains. Your seniors will appreciate your efforts. 'Page of Cups' indicates that you need to take advice form people who are experienced and more knowledgeable. It will help you in decision making. If waiting for results, you are likely to get positive outcomes. You will get spiritual this week and take out time for yourself. 'Three of Swords' says that you can create doubts and problems for yourself if you don't work in a meaningful and in a confident manner.

Love
There seems some misunderstandings in love paradise this week. There could be some conflicts which need to be sorted out by devoting some time.

Money
You will be more free and relaxed as far as your finances are concerned this week.

Health
Health is a high matter of concern this week. Strict advice from doctor is recommended even if minor health problems strike you.

Career
Career seems to be on the right track as you are enthusiastic and eager for taking up work this week.

Education
You are highly intelligent as you are analyzing and evaluating each and every step that you take. This will

help you find better solutions and upgrade your IQ level on time.

Lucky numbers
3 and 9

Lucky colour
Magenta Pink

Lucky days
Sunday, Monday and Friday

Remedies
You have to understand the feelings of the people around you. You need to project yourself in a better and a mature way. Keep aside your ego and attitude and accept suggestions from others. You can consult an expert and take advice from him/her. Your life will change for the better if you include more people and their ideas in your life.

35th Week
(August 23 to 29)

Overview
'Queen of Swords' suggests that you are not fully utilizing your intellect. Make sure that while using your intellect, you divert all your energy so as to evaluate the situations from all aspects. Do not get showy as there is a tendency being indicated. Do not over spend this week,

though you can go out and enjoy the pleasure which satisfy your wants. You have to avoid people who can have a negative influence. Don't let your emotions take over your mind while taking decisions. Be more mature but do not trust any third person blindly. Offers will come and go from your hand this week, you need to be specific and take advantage of these offers. Whenever you take up a new path, make sure that you have deep and full-fledged knowledge about it and then implement your plans. Do not blindly move ahead as it can harm your aim and destination. Your immaturity or childlike nature can force you to take up many tasks at a time about which you do not even have knowledge. Be careful and take advice wherever needed. These problems will vanish as you are determined and you will take all the devotion and the necessary steps in order to clear out these obstacles. After all the hurdles and competition, you will be the winner at the end of the week

Love
'Three of Pentacles' says that you will be getting support from a third person this week. You will be happy to get this support and help.

Money
'Seven of Cups' says that money prospects are looking nice but surely can be improved by taking advantage of the offers that come your way.

Health
'Ace of Cups' says that your health will be enjoyable this week.

Career
'Five of Cups' says that you can be thinking about a recent setback in career, but in order to move ahead you have to take a step ahead.

Education
You have to accept the offer that is coming your way. Be more action oriented and responsive.

Lucky numbers
5 and 6

Lucky colour
Sea Green

Lucky days
Sunday, Tuesday and Saturday

Remedies
You have to forget the past and move on in life so as to achieve more success. Keep on working and keep putting in your energy in the same frequency and pace. You won't be able to move forward if you don't take the right steps at the right time. You can keep a pair of Dolphin fishes on your office desk for your career enhancement. You can even place a Bamboo plant on your table at home or in your office.

36th Week
(August 30 to September 5)

Overview
'Knight of Cups' says that you will be focused as far as your tasks are concerned and at the same time, you will not neglect your family needs and their wants. There is a balance maintained. A journey is being indicated this week. You have to be more expressive and interactive this week. The interactions can bring more offers or bright chances where you can get a chance to prove your abilities. Meet more people or go for a reunion party this week. You will be ready to make a move and take one step ahead. You are high on energy and enthusiasm. You may feel that situations are getting stagnant. The reason is that you are investing at this time whereas investment is one of the priorities. 'The World' indicates that you have all the blessings you need. You can start new work in case you are planning to. Do not get egoistic or doubtful as some third person can take advantage of this situation and lead the race. You will be creating a problem for yourself. 'The Hanged Man' says that you will get spiritual this week. But you need to devote more time thinking about the decisions that you take. Do not get indecisive instead believe in your instincts and move ahead.

Love
You will be attracted towards your lover this week.

Singles can get committed if planning to as positive response is indicated.

Money
Money needs attention, as there are chances of you to get possessive this week. Help the needy as they need your support and helping hand.

Health
You will be celebrating your good health. This is a perfect week for your health.

Career
'Four of Pentacles' says that you need to come out from set mind frame and accept changes as you see them. It will be beneficial for you.

Education
'Knight of Pentacles' says that you are likely to create hurdles for yourself if you do not take the right steps to increase your awareness.

Lucky numbers
6 and 7

Lucky colour
Maroon

Lucky days
Sunday, Tuesday and Thursday

Remedies
You have to meet more people and remove the rigidness.

Be more flexible and adapt to changes as you face them. Spend the needed amount of money in the right direction. Fulfill all your desires on time as it will give you a sense of satisfaction. You can even wear a metal Kada on your left hand as it will help you become more responsible and committed.

37th Week
(September 6 to 12)

Overview
'The Temperance' says that your focus and temperament allows you to strike a balance between your work and personal life. You will be getting spiritual this week. You have to be careful as there is an indication of a sudden loss. You need to take utmost care before taking any decision. 'King of Cups' says that you will be highly emotional but not ready to project and advertise your emotions. You need to be expressive so as to carry out meaningful conversations. You are intelligently putting in all the needed efforts in the right direction. You will be financially benefited this week. This is the right time to take investment decisions. You can expect a delay in your work, but the delay will benefit you in the future. Make sure your mind doesn't get diverted. You shall not overload yourself with additional pressure. Your health can get affected this week. Be positive and give proper guidance as you are

likely to enjoy a good status at home and at office. Make use of your experience this week.

Love
'Eight of Cups' says you are likely to leave behind all emotions this week. In this way, there can be a communication gap which needs to be avoided.

Money
Money prospects need care as you are unable to concentrate on your finances this week. Make proper utilization

Health
'The Devil' suggests that overloading yourself can make you feel week and unhealthy. Take rest this week.

Career
'Ace of Wands' says that your career chart will go up this week as you are expected to get the work of your choice.

Education
'The Tower' says that education can see a downfall if not paid attention to. Take every possible chance to enhance your education.

Lucky numbers
5 and 8

Lucky colour
Earthly Brown

Lucky days
Monday, Wednesday and Saturday

Remedies
You can be deceived as someone is trying to take undue advantage of you. You can wear a black Tourmaline pendant this week, which will help you escape all black magic and negativity. The evil effects will not reach you. Seems you have got hurt regarding a relation. You have to forget the past and move ahead as life has many things to be explored.

38th Week
(September 13 to 19)

Overview
You will get positive outcomes and the results that your hard work deserves. Positive outcomes are coming your way. You can get possessive and selfish regarding your financial status. Help the people who need your assistance. 'Four of Wands' indicates that your pending work can get over if you willingly take up those tasks. In this way, as the old work gets over, you can start and initiate new tasks too. You will be on the right track by implementing your views and plans at the right time. You are ready to work hard too. 'The Death' says that you may experience the situations taking a drastic turn and a big change is yet to take place. You will be energetic and excited regarding a new venture. Things

will fall on your lap as you are working towards your goal with dedication. You will be getting emotional support from a near one. Spouse/partner will be helping you this week. By the end of the week, you will be helping others with their problems. People will seek your guidance and help.

Love
'The Sun' says that you will be the one who hold authority and charge in relationships this week.

Money
'Six of Wands' says that money prospects are very bright as you are able to concentrate on your finances and take the right decisions.

Health
'The Emperor' says that your health is likely to get affected if you take unnecessary steps to help others.

Career
Career front will be good this week. You are likely to get the work matching your expectations and interest.

Education
You will be high on education this week, without giving any complaints. People will even look up to you for guidance.

Lucky numbers
2 and 4

Lucky colour
Lotus Pink

Lucky days
Monday, Friday and Saturday

Remedies
You need to be thankful to God for all that you have received till now. You have to make a routine to pray in front of God for your wellbeing. You need to take blessings from God and your elders. You can even keep a photo of God.

39th Week
(September 20 to 26)

Overview
'The Emperor' indicates that you have to take care of your priorities before you start helping others. You need to realize that you have everything that you need in front of you. But you have to cut the black swirl; which is around you so that you are easily accessible to these benefits. You have to make decisions beforehand this week, as you can face a dilemma which will leave you in confusion. You need to have patience this week. You are likely to get attracted towards someone special which will leave you romantic. Take care of your tasks as there is a downfall being indicated this week, if you continue to work for others without realizing you aim.

'Ten of Pentacles' indicates that you have to get more active regarding the financial decisions that you make this week. Do not get egoistic as it can hurt others and this can even hamper your path and destination. 'Ace of Swords' says that at the end you will be the one who will enjoy the fruits and success. You have to keep your focus intact and your determination should not take a turn to the negative.

Love
You will be committed and responsible towards your partner/spouse. Singles may come to know that someone is interested in them.

Money
'Eight of Pentacles' says that your hard-earned money can go to waste if you do not attend to it properly. Spend some part of your income on yourself this week.

Health
'Ten of Wands' says that you can affect your health, if you overload or overburden yourself with unnecessary worries and concern. Be careful and concentrate on the needed aspects of life.

Career
You have to be action-oriented so that you get to work upon the offers that you receive.

Education
'Seven of Wands' says that you are ready to work hard

this week. And this attitude of yours will help you gain more information and knowledge. This is a good time for students as they will be able to concentrate more.

Lucky numbers
1 and 7

Lucky colour
Maroon

Lucky days
Sunday, Wednesday and Saturday

Remedies
This week, you need to spend money on yourself. You are a self-made person who also has the right to enjoy life using all the pleasures. There is a need for new enhancements in all aspects of life. You will be able to reach your aim on time providing you work with positive attitude. You need to plan out an outing and take out time for yourself and your family. You can even go for shopping this week.

40th Week
(September 27 to October 3)

Overview
You will get victory, if stuck in any legal matters as you are likely to get the benefit of doubt and you will go on winning hearts. You can get showy this week, as you

are likely to earn monetary benefits. Avoid over expenditure this week. 'Nine of Swords' says that do not get indecisive this week by being firm. You need to take help whenever needed. Support from your loved ones will give confidence. You have to focus hard and surrender yourself to your work and task so that the results come out as expected. You are likely to get passionate regarding your love life and you will definitely get the needed support. You are heading towards your destination with full power and vigor this week. Your power will help you reach your aims on time. You are highly focused this week with all powers being balanced between your personal and professional life. Do not work on a probability basis, as it can hamper and spoil your path by giving you unwanted tension.

Love
Love matters need attention as there is sudden misunderstanding or dispute being indicated. Be interactive and avoid all scope for such misunderstandings.

Money
Finances will be high on priority this week and you need to take proper steps so as to save the money for future expenses.

Health
Health will be fine as you will take all steps to be fit and healthy.

Career
'Five of Wands' says that career will demand a lot of attention as there is competition being indicated this week at the work place.

Education
You have to concentrate on your upgradation instead of enhancing and helping others with their education. You may get a setback if you do not change your attitude and concentrating on your work.

Lucky numbers
2 and 6

Lucky colour
Grey

Lucky days
Sunday, Wednesday and Friday

Remedies
Your career and love needs care this week. Put in more efforts for meaningful work and positive results. You can do some charity work or preparing a Wealth vase (the preparation of wealth vase is mentioned at the back of the book). You have to be practical and during this week, you can even take help from others.

41st Week
(October 4 to 10)

Overview

You need to gain full knowledge before you actually implement all your plans as there is negligence being indicated. You have to make sure that all your plans are according to the need of the situation. Do not be shy or ignorant as it can prove harmful to your intentions and goals. You have to take the needful steps by meeting new people and exchanging your ideas and views with them. 'Temperance' says that your focus and temperament allows you to strike a balance between your work and personal life. You will be getting spiritual this week. You might tackle up many tasks at a time without having full knowledge about each. You have to have clarity of thought before taking up any particular job. You will be cheerful and excited about a recent income or work. This will keep you active through the mid-week. You need to take advantage of this activeness and make a move forward. 'Seven of Cups' says that you need to enjoy all the elements and resources that you see in front of you. You have to make full and better utilization of the available inputs. 'Three of Swords' indicates that you may create self-created obstacles for yourself by doubting your own capabilities and potentials. You need to have confidence on your abilities and move ahead without being egoistic or doubtful.

You will aim higher as time moves on. This will be beneficial for you and you will be more successful.

Love
Love life is looking highly bright as all your energy is diverted towards your partner and you will be emotionally satisfied this week.

Money
'The Hierophant' says that you will be in a mood to help others this week through your resources and inputs.

Health
Health seems to be little affected as you are not taking proper medication or steps to be fit and healthy. Follow the routine as prescribed by the doctor.

Career
Career will be satisfying this week, as you have the blessings and the courage to move ahead.

Education
You shall not doubt your capabilities. In this way, you are actually helping others move ahead of you. You have to be careful this week regarding education.

Lucky numbers
3 and 5

Lucky colour
Turquoise Blue

134 / CAPRICORN

Lucky days
Monday, Thursday and Saturday

Remedies
Wealth and education needs attention. Do not doubt on anybody. You have to adapt yourself to the new technology and get used to it from time to time. You can enhance your surroundings with Yellow colour this week. Light Yellow candles everyday for 5 minutes for well-being and clarity of mind.

42nd Week
(October 11 to 17)

Overview
'The Empress' suggests that you will start this week by satisfying the wants of people who have helped you achieve your targets. You will act as a pillar of strength to many people. Do not over-burden yourself this week by taking on additional stress and work on your shoulders. You have to learn to say No to people. Invest the money that comes your way as it will yield fruitful returns. You will come out on top and shine as bright as the star. People will be impressed with your presence of mind and creativity. 'Queen of Swords' says that you need to utilize your intellect fully so that your energy do not go to waste. Make sure you do not get deviated from your path as there are chances this week. You need to keep your focus intact and go on without looking

back. 'The Fool' shows us that as the weekend approaches, you will be elated and excited. Your carefree nature may force you to try new things this weekend. A third person will come to your help when you are in a difficult situation. You will appreciate the efforts and support of this person.

Love
You have to be more action oriented and take care of the fact that your loved ones are not in a difficult situation. You have to act as their pillar of support.

Money
You have to mix with people and try to avoid getting tensed. You need to divert your mind. Take practical decisions after consultation.

Health
Health will be at its best this week. Try enjoying your hobbies this week.

Career
Career will be enjoyable this week. You will be spending your time by evaluating your performance till now.

Education
You can become negative and transfer all your energy towards someone without being able to concentrate on your education enhancement. You have to stay positive and take advantage of all the benefits that come your way.

Lucky numbers
1 and 3

Lucky colour
White

Lucky days
Tuesday, Friday and Saturday

Remedies
You have to concentrate on your finances this week. You are ready to give your money and someone is trying to take advantage of this attitude of yours. You shall give but not by sacrificing your needs. Plan your budget this week or you can even take help of someone who can manage your accounts and finances.

43rd Week
(October 18 to 24)

Overview
You have to be highly practical and calm when you face difficult situations. You have the determination and the willpower to move ahead by crossing all these hurdles. You will get a lot of time to enjoy with your family and friends. You will get a much needed rest and time off from your work. You will use all your talents and experience in your work and this gives you hope and faith in your abilities. 'King of Pentacles' says that

you might get possessive regarding your monetary benefits. You have to help during this period as your worth will be counted during this time only. Do not go away from your emotional bondages. These might give some conflicts and confusions in your mind. You have to respect relations this week and you will surely get the needed support from your family members. Students who are awaiting results will get positive news. You will be full of positive vibe this week as you get to hear good news. You will be highly pleased with the benefits you will get now. You will be ready to work for others and help them with their work. 'Six of Wands' says that you will be applauded and the hype will give you a positive boost and force to work even harder.

Love
You have to be careful and tactful while having discussions with your loved ones.

Money
'The Magician' says that you will be managing your finances very well as you have a magic wand in your hand and you will make full utilization of the power and authority this week.

Health
Health will be fantastic as it will support your career and personal life. Overall this week is good for enjoying your hobbies and other activities.

Career
You will be concentrating on your task this week. You are likely to get work of your interest and qualification.

Education
You will be highly encouraged to take up a course or make a move so as to enhance and improve your knowledge.

Lucky numbers
9 and 10

Lucky colour
Deep Red

Lucky days
Sunday, Friday and Saturday

Remedies
You are likely to become over-confident and your ego can hurt others. There is an indication of over-involvement either in a habit or in a relation this week. Do not take decisions being one sided. You will be the ultimate winner and to achieve that target you need to believe in yourself and do not get dependent on others. You can wear a Red stone or keep a Red cloth with yourself so as to feel more energized. In this way there will also be harmony and balance in your life.

44th Week
(October 25 to 31)

Overview

'Seven of Swords' says that the week can start on a low note as you are taking up decisions and responsibilities in the wrong direction. This may be because someone had mislead you. But you need to take advice from a trustworthy person. You have to be decisive and take steps to invest and roll on your money in the right direction on time. You will be analytical and evaluative this week which prepares you for the future difficulties and obstacles. Be more open with the people as exchange of views and interaction is the key word now. You need to please people by your creative and imaginative powers. You have to forget the past and move ahead by holding your present in the correct manner. You will get to hear news because of which you will celebrate and enjoy the mid week, a party can be held and enjoyed. 'Eight of Pentacles' says that you can get possessive as now you are not willing to spend the hard-earned money on yourself. You have to be little spendthrift this week and enjoy using your money. 'The Chariot' indicates that you may go on a short journey which will help you get spiritual or learn new things.

Love

This is the perfect time when you can initiate new relations as your inclination is towards someone special. This is a very enjoyable and memorable time for people who are thinking for a deeper commitment.

Money
'Page of Wands' says that you will be financially stable as you are working in the right manner so as to earn more gains.

Health
You have to get accustomed to the changes that you notice in your environment. Otherwise your stubborn nature can make you ill and weak this week.

Career
Money is going to come this week through your job and this way you will be content and happier. Your career graph is going in the way you wanted it to move.

Education
You have to be more action oriented and responsive so that you take up the offers that come your way this week. You need to improve your awareness by reading newspapers or magazines.

Lucky numbers
4 and 8

Lucky colour
Chocolate Brown

Lucky days
Monday, Friday and Saturday

Remedies

You need to understand that too much of discipline is also not good in life. You have to accept things and situations as they come. You can wear a Five mukhi Rudraksh as it will prevent you from taking decisions in an immature way. There will be an overall balance and you will also enjoy good health.

45th Week
(November 1 to 7)

Overview

You may get indecisive at the beginning of this week. You need to have patience and confidence in yourself. God will help you and show you the right path. 'Two of Pentacles' says that you are likely to come across some offers and money which will even pass your way if not paid attention to. Be careful and take keen interest in your surroundings. You have to avoid mingling with people who have a negative influence on you. You have to be influential this week. 'Six of Cups' says that you are likely to help people and behave like a pillar of support for the needy. You will be able to satisfy people's expectations. 'Ace of Pentacles says that you can make a huge investment this week, if planning. You will be benefited if money is spent on property. You need not help others by wasting all your energy. You are likely to get very less returns. You will be highly focused and determined and at the same time you will even devote time to your family. There is a balance being maintained. You will be bright and the centre of attraction wherever you go this week. Your friends will enjoy your company and support. The week-end is on a very high note.

Love
You may get highly motivated or attracted towards a person which can leave you in no man's land. All the other aspects of life will be affected if same attitude is continued.

Money
Money management is poor this week. If proper guidance is not followed then you can face a deep trouble. Keep yourself calm and move ahead steadily. Patience is the key word this week.

Health
'Knight of Wands' indicates that you will be on your toes as you are energetic and this will reflect in your health too leaving you healthy.

Career
'Ace of Wands' says that career will be fantastic this week. You are highly satisfied with your career path. This is an amazing week to start of with a new place or job.

Education
'The Tower' suggests that if you do not make up for the

last time by improving your knowledge and awareness, you can suffer a setback. You need to work for yourself now instead of sacrificing for others.

Lucky numbers
4 and 6

Lucky colour
Black

Lucky days
Wednesday, Thursday and Saturday

Remedies
There are too many ups and downs being indicated this week. You have to be calm otherwise; your blood pressure can take a toll by getting hyper-tensed. Health needs attention. You may commit mistakes by being over-responsible and over-loading yourself. There will be changes in your life for betterment now. You can tie a Black thread on your right hand. This will help you avoid all negative energy and you will be able to adjust yourself to the changing environment.

46th Week
(November 8 to 14)

Overview
You have to be practical this week by avoiding to meet people who have a negative eye on you and your work.

You can get affected negatively and it may also hamper your performance. Check out the resources and elements that you have in front of you. You will have to cut down the black swirl and take full advantage of the situations that you face. 'The High Priestess' says that you need to work upon your capabilities and talents so as to get some meaningful results. Come out of the fixed mind set so that you get to experience the changes that are taking place in your surroundings. You will be benefited if you change your attitude. You will get lots of gains this week which give you a much needed boost of energy and vibe with which you will plan for future. Make sure that these gains are being put to the right use. You can plan to invest in share market too. 'Queen of Pentacles' says that you may get showy due to these recent gains. Avoid over expenditure this week. Your positive force will help you take up new responsibilities this week. Keep the focus as it can take you to new heights.

Love
You will get positive response if awaiting someone's response or answer. You will have an impressive effect on others this week.

Money
Though you may come across some small hurdles you are likely to surpass them using your wit and intelligence.

Health
'Death Card' says that you will see some transformations taking place. You need to take utmost care of your health so that it does not get worse.

Career
You will get justice in all the fields wherever you have invested your time money and energy.

Education
Your focus and determination will be paid this week. Students who are planning to go for higher studies will get positive results.

Lucky numbers
2 and 7

Lucky colour
Dark Green

Lucky days
Sunday, Wednesday and Thursday

Remedies
You need to use more of whites in your routine this week. You can wear White clothes and also include green leafy vegetables in your diet. This will help you maintain good health and give you prosperity. You can even feed cattle with fodder. You will be encouraged to work harder.

47th Week
(November 15 to 21)

Overview
'Knight of Pentacles' indicates that the week may start on a stagnant note. You are not ready to put in the desired inputs and in this way, you may see that things are not moving. A person either at the work place or at home is likely to ditch you and take undue advantage of your honesty. Be clear with your terms and conditions so that there is no scope left for others to take advantage of you. There will be a person in your life who will willingly come to your help and service. You will be delighted with this effort. 'The Tower' says that your sacrificing nature can pull you down from your position and in this way you can suffer a set-back. You have to use your positive enthusiasm in the right direction so as to yield maximum benefits. 'Nine of Cups' says that you will spend some time in evaluating gains and performance. You will be satisfied with your performance. Your incomplete work will be completed if you take them again. You can even initiate new projects this week. 'The Magician' shows us that you will be the highlight at every social event this weekend. You will even enhance your public relations in this way.

Love
You have to take action and spend more time with your family this week. Your near ones seek your support.

Money
You have to take up the offer that is coming your way. You will be benefited if you work upon these offers using your money.

Health
You will be enjoying a very good health and you can even satisfy all your hobbies and take up other activities.

Career
You will try and help others but for less profits. You need to understand and prioritize your tasks and work towards them.

Education
You will be enthusiastic about a recent venture. You will take full pride in your studies and you will definitely get positive results.

Lucky numbers
1 and 9

Lucky colour
Mustered Yellow

Lucky days
Monday, Friday and Saturday

Remedies
Do not get over-possessive this week regarding your work and relations. In this way, you may not be able to move ahead too. You are busy in rolling on your money

in the right direction. For completion of life cycle, you need to take blessings from your elders by respecting them and spending time with them. You will get emotional stability if you can keep a Rose Quartz with yourself. Devote more time to your partner/spouse.

48th Week
(November 22 to 28)

Overview

Do not over-pressurize yourself by taking wrong decisions without proper support from your seniors. You need some time off so that you can do some self appraisal. You will have the blessings from all the masculine and feminine powers which show you the path where you can start a new journey. Do not get inclined or motivated towards a particular task as due to this, you can even neglect all other responsibilities. Check your priorities this week and make the right move as far as your investments are concerned. You will be known in a better and profound way this week among your colleagues. Do not avoid taking advantage of the opportunities that come your way. Forget the lost things or relations and move ahead with what you hold in your hand. Be analytical in such a way that you get to know an overview of the situation on the whole. You will get more success if you understand the situation more deeply. 'Ace of Wands' says that a new beginning is being indicated this week as far as your career or education enhancement is concerned. You will get success in the new project that you take up.

Love

You will be highly satisfied and you will even start to settle down with a recent relationship. You may see that your relations are improving.

Money

You have to be careful while dealing with money matters. Take deep interest and acquire full knowledge before signing any deal.

Health

You may be sad as others are not listening to you. But you should not let this behaviour of others' affect your health.

Career

You will see a new direction this week. You will be ready to implement your plans and take up this new assignment with pride.

Education

Do not doubt on your abilities instead have faith and move ahead with confidence.

Lucky numbers
4 and 7

Lucky colour
Green

Lucky days
Sunday, Wednesday and Saturday

Remedies
You have to surrender yourself to God and the task that you take up. You will get more prosperity if you work with willingness. You need to be polite and not impulsive. You will get positive results if you work according to the situations. You can even invite your friend over for a get-together and acquire more knowledge by interaction.

49th Week
(November 29 to December 5)

Overview
'Queen of Cups' says that you have to be more positive this week without getting influenced by the people who are around you. You have to be rather influential. Try and be more mind-oriented instead of heart oriented. You will definitely see the change, if you change your emotional attitude to a stronger character. 'The Stars' says that all your dreams will be fulfilled this week. You have the blessings of your elders and you will succeed in all aspects of life. Though you are taking care of your relatives and juniors, you need to be more responsive and show your feelings towards your loved ones. They should come to know about your feelings so that there are no misunderstandings. Enjoy your self-

earned name and fame this week. Do not let go any opportunity where you get to utilize your money in a positive way. You will be in a celebration mood. You can call all your friends for a party this week and enjoy time. 'Seven of Pentacles' says that you have to be more action-oriented so that your money is rolled on and you get to enjoy more fruits. You will act as a guide and help your juniors with your knowledge and experiences. You will try and show the correct path to the ones who need your support. 'Five of Pentacles' indicates that the week could end on a low note due to a sudden loss if precautions are not taken beforehand. Do not sign any deal without reading the terms and conditions clearly.

Love
Love life is looking tremendously bright as your emotional needs will be satisfied. Singles can take a further step towards a deeper commitment.

Money
'Eight of Cups' says that you may move away from your relations but these difficulties will keep on hovering your mind. Take out time and think deeply with the help of guidance regarding your money matters.

Health
You have to take care of your health as work pressure can affect you. Consult the doctor even if you are stuck with minor ailments.

Career
You will be getting all the support of your juniors and colleagues. You will work with full dedication and passion.

Education
You will take all possible advantage from the opportunities that you get. You will be happy with the way your education gets enhanced.

Lucky numbers
3 and 8

Lucky colour
Ocean Blue

Lucky days
Sunday, Wednesday and Friday

Remedies
You are on the right path for earning money. You shall not do any job which makes you feel guilty or down. You can give some donation from a part of your income to the old age home or the orphan's society. You will get blessings and you will be able to work with more heart and mind in your work.

50th Week
(December 6 to 12)

Overview
'The Empress' says that you will take out time for others this week. You will be focusing all your energy towards helping and supporting others. You will be analytical and evaluative and this attitude will prepare you for the future situations. Be more specific while talking and exchanging your views with others. You can be taken for a ride this week. You need to make sure that whenever you work, you put in the entire needed efforts so that you get maximum results. You are likely to get romantic during the midweek as your focus now turns from your work to your relations. 'Knight of Wands' says that you will be rearing to move ahead with a positive force and a focused mind. You will be high on the emotional sector and you will surely get the desired results. You will be facing competition at the work place or at school. You have to grab this opportunity and work with full dedication.

Love
You will get all that you need and want this week. You will be on a high as you will see all your wants being fulfilled.

Money
Money and finances are looking high on priority. You will gain lots of money due to your work.

Health
Forgetting the past will be the medicine to your weakness this week. You have to move ahead by letting go the past.

Career
You have to make realistic decisions this week. You have to have faith in God and he will show you the right path.

Education
You have to be open as this will only help you improve and enhance your education prospects.

Lucky numbers
1 and 5

Lucky colour
Peacock Blue

Lucky days
Sunday, Wednesday and Thursday

Remedies
Your career needs time so that you can arrive at firm conclusions. Do not close yourself in a grid. There is the need for upgradation of knowledge and education from your environment. You need to be more organized, planned and disciplined. You can place a Red showpiece in your room in the south east direction so that you can work with more vigor and power.

51st Week
(December 13 to 19)

Overview

'Five of Swords' says that knocking your hand at every door will do no good to you. You have to work with perfection. So take up one challenge at a time. Your helping and supporting nature will get you a good name. You will be famous at the social sector. Be ready to take an investment project. You can even try and invest in property or in the share market. You may get egoistic and doubtful but your ego can either hurt someone or help someone to take the charge. You can even lose the race if you do not keep aside your ego. 'Two of Swords' says that being aloof and lonely will hamper your aims. You have to meet new people and have an interaction and projection of your thoughts in front of them. You will get positive hope from such interactions. 'Page of Swords' says that getting into a path without even having knowledge about that particular path will get you in trouble. You need to acquire full and deep knowledge before you move ahead by implementing your plans. You will get positive judgment if awaiting any results. Students will score good marks in their examinations and this will act as a boost to their confidence. 'The Temperance' says that you will be able to maintain a focus and determination while completing a task this week.

Love
'Ten of Cups' says that you will take out time for your love and personal life this week.

Money
You will enjoy your financial position and make effective utilization of your gains.

Health
You will be very healthy and enjoy good atmosphere this week. You will be at mental peace.

Career
You will be cheerful and ecstatic regarding the work you are likely to get this week.

Education
You do not have to overload yourself with unnecessary information. You can get stressed. You need to take a break this week.

Lucky numbers
1 and 2

Lucky colour
Purple

Lucky days
Sunday, Monday and Friday

Remedies
You are moving too fast this week. In this way, you may not notice the changes in your environment. You have

to move slowly and steadily by taking one step at a time otherwise you can fall down from your current position.

52nd Week
(December 20 to 26)

Overview
You need to enjoy the fruits of the hard work that you have done. You are a self made person. So enjoy all the gains before it's too late. You will use all your intellect and experience in the right direction. You will succeed if you take up a new job during this week. You may experience an overall new situation that you now face. There will be a transformation in the moments that you now experience. You can experience offers and money coming and going from your hands. Grab the best offer and start working upon it. Investment is needed if you are ready to take up new work otherwise you may feel stagnant this week. 'The Tower' suggests that you can fall from a current position if you do not stop sacrificing for others. You have to take out time for yourself and evaluate your performance before it's too late. Be interactive and responsive this week so that you get a chance to take advantage of the ideas you come across. You will work towards your aim with full power and force. You will get the desired results.

Love
'Seven of Cups' says that though you have all the

happiness in the world, you are unable to see and realize it. You will be able to realize it only when you take out time for your relations.

Money
You will be ready to take up responsibilities by implementing your inputs and plans and money at the right time.

Health
Health needs time as you have to take out time for yourself this week.

Career
Career needs attention as some one is trying to take advantage of you at the work front. Be careful while dealing with people.

Education
You have to work with full force instead on probability basis and make sure that you improve your knowledge with time.

Lucky numbers
2 and 4

Lucky colour
Almond Brown

Lucky days
Sunday, Tuesday and Saturday

Remedies

You have to trust yourself and in your abilities. Do not expect from others but concentrate on your work. You have to keep an eye on your steps and what others are doing for you. Everything will be fine if you move ahead with full energy and power. Do not question yourself too much. Sometimes, over analysis can end in paralysis. Enhance your surroundings with Red colour for more zeal and enthusiasm.

53rd Week
(December 27 to January 2)

Overview

'The Lovers' says that in the beginning of the week, you will get highly romantic and devote your time towards your loved one. You will see all your dreams coming true this week. You have to make arrangements so that you take up the correct investment project. 'Knight of Swords' indicates that you need to be more slow and steady before you take up any project. Do not move in a hurry so as to finish all the tasks without perfection. You may have to be diplomatic this week at the work place so that your work does not stop in mid. You have to open up so that people get to know about your ideas and plans and you also get a chance to project your views. You will definitely be benefited with these interactions. 'Page of Pentacles' says that your carefree nature and attitude will help you yield and attract more people towards you.

Love
'The Chariot' says that a new relation will start of at a very positive note.

Money
'Two of Wands' says that you will see inflow of offers through which you can make future arrangements using your money.

Health
You will be enjoying your health all through this week as you may take out time to rest.

Career
This week, you have to grab the opportunity that you get and also work upon it so that you get the apt chance to show your talents in the true form.

Education
You need to work in order to upgrade your knowledge without worrying about the results. The obstacles that you face will easily be removed by using your intellect.

Lucky numbers
7 and 8

Lucky colour
White

Lucky days
Sunday, Monday and Thursday

Remedies
You have to take steps with confidence because if you fear failure you will not be able to move ahead at all. You will get justice if you move with a positive frame of mind. Do not get suspicious instead have faith in your heart and mind. You can keep a Yellow garland at the temple and pray for your wellbeing and good health.

REMEDIES

1. Wealth-vase

The Wealth-vase enhances your monetary position with time. It can be made as follows-

You need to take a clear vase which would contain the picture of Goddess Laxmi on the upper side of the vase (it should be placed in such a manner that Goddess Laxmi is having a look at the bottom of the vase).

Three Chinese coins tied with a Red ribbon need to be placed inside the vase.

Fill half of the vase with semi-precious stones of seven types.

You also need to bring some quantity of mud or soil from a person whom you think is a rich person.

Place Red money or Coins in a Red packet and place it in the vase.

Next, you need to place five types of seeds or grains (wheat, rice, jowar, baajra and maize)

You also need to place ten small crystal balls in the Wealth-vase for stability.

Then papers in yellow, red, white, blue and green colour need to be cut in pieces and then kept at the bottom of the vase.

This Wealth-vase should be placed in the south-east direction of the house in such a manner that it is visible only to you and not to outsiders.

2. Vishnu Kalash

For the Vishnu Kalash the following has to be done:

Take a Copper Vessel (vase is acceptable) and place Silver coins in it on which the picture of Lord Ganesh and Goddess Laxmi are embedded.

The coins need to be placed in such a manner that the picture should be visible from the top of the mouth of the vase.

Fill the vase with water and change the water everyday.

Place Ashoka leaves and a coconut over it.

The Vishnu Kalash needs to be placed at the north-east direction of the house.

The Vishnu Kalash is also an effective way of enhancing the monetary position of the house.

3. Charity

Charity includes any kind of charity which would help you yield blessings and good wishes. You can go ahead and donate the following so as to enhance your week by doing good deeds.

- Donate books and sponsor education of a child and make a child study
- You can go ahead and even feed a needy and satisfy his/her need
- Donation involving clothes are also a very good way of making someone happy

4. Harmonic Star

'The Harmonic Star' says that you can go ahead and serve humanity. According to this, you will receive only those results aback for the work that you do. You can proceed in making the Harmonic Star by cutting the paper and making it 3 by 3. Then fold it in such a way that it becomes double and make a triangle out of it. The pin point which proceeds from the south to the north indicates that it is Humanity to God and the pin point which goes from the north to south says that it is what you receive from God. You will get what you do and thus, you should concentrate on only good deeds always. One should always say and perform good things without hurting or harming anyone.

5. Crystal

The Crystal signifies balance and stability in life. One who is facing upheavals in life can make use of any Crystal show-piece or ball and make life better and more stable. The Crystal should be placed either at the centre of the house if there is instability at the home place or at the office table if you need stability there.

Crystal involves the following objects which can affect your life in a positive way:
1. Crystal Ball
2. Crystal Shree Yantra
3. Crystal Show-piece
4. Crystal Lotus

5. Crystal Pyramid
6. Crystal Necklace
7. Crystal Pencils

These objects will help you bring more stability and much needed balance in life and will help you look at things from a better perspective.

6. Rock salt

The use of Rock salt in our daily life will help you prevent the effect from negative vibrations that pass on from others. The Rock salt will help to absorb all the negativity from the environment around you and will help you lead a positive life. You can place a bowl full of salt in your bath room. You can sweep the floor once a week with salt water and clean the house with it so that it takes away all the negativity from your surrounding. The utilization of Rock salt is an effective way of eliminating negativity from your house.

7. Wish pyramid

The Wish Pyramid is an effective way from which you will see your wishes coming true or close to coming true. You will have confidence and faith in your abilities and you will focus on working towards your aim in the right direction. For the Wish Pyramid you need to do the following:

On a White sheet of paper you need to write down your wish with a Red pen and place it in a box which will be known as the Wish Pyramid. The wish has to be read everyday three times so that you remind yourself of your aim and continuously work towards the attainment of your aim and goals.

8. Colours
(a) Red
The Red colour is the colour of energy and vitality. The use of Red colour in our daily lives will give us the needed enthusiasm which will push us and help us to work towards our aim. You can use Red colour in your dressing style and also light Red candles everyday for 3-5 minutes as it will empower you with energy. You can even use Red fruits in your daily diet.

(b) Blue
The Blue colour brings enhancement in your career and education life. The use of Blue colour at home or at office premises will help you lead a better life at the career or at the education. You can enhance your surroundings with Blue colour by using it in your dressing style. You can also place a pair of Dolphin fishes or Madeline ducks. Placing the fountain at the office will help you give a smooth flow in your career life.

(c) Green
Green colour implies monetary enhancement and prosperity. The Green colour will give you the much

needed happiness in all prospects. You can use Green colour in your daily diet by including green leafy vegetables in your diet. You can even wear Green dresses and enhance your day with vitality and prosperity.

(d) Yellow
The Yellow colour gives you clarity in your thoughts and mind process. Yellow colour will give you the courage to arrive at the right decision at the right time. You can use Yellow colour in your daily use and also in your fruit intake.

(e) Orange
Orange colour gives you strength and courage to move forward with a clear and a focused mind. You will get the power to move ahead and take the right steps. Lighting Orange colour candles will give a positive vibe in your environment and make you stronger.

(f) Purple
The Purple colour emphasizes on spirituality and divination. People who want to introduce a deeper content of spiritualism into their lives can use more of Purple colour in their lives and make a go.

(g) Pink
Pink colour indicates relations. Those who are going through a rough patch in their relations can make use

of Pink and give a positive turn to their problems. You can use Pink Rose Quartz in your daily routine to enhance your life. You can even use Pink colour by wearing Pink colour dresses and also lighting Pink candles everyday for 3-5 minutes which will help you get positive energy.